HEIDELBERG SCIENCE LIBRARY | Volume 11

Computers, Chess and Long-Range Planning

M. M. Botvinnik

Translated by Arthur Brown

Springer-Verlag
New York•Heidelberg•Berlin | 1970

© 1970 by Springer-Verlag New York Inc. Library of Congress Catalog Number 75-85203
Printed in the United States of America

Title Number 3920

Contents

Translator's Preface

Mihail Moiseevich Botvinnik is an electrical engineer by profession; during World War II he headed a high-tension laboratory in the Urals and was decorated by the USSR for his accomplishments. At present, he is the head of the alternating-current machine laboratory at the Moscow Institute of Power Engineering. He is also a world-renowned chess player. He was born in 1911, and by 1935 had become a Grandmaster of Soviet chess. In 1948 he won the world chess championship and held the title until 1963 (except for a two-year break).

His chess style has been characterized as deep, objective, serious, and courageous. In this book, the quality of his thinking is revealed in his study of the basic thought processes of master chess players, and his reduction of these processes to mathematical form. This formalization of thought processes is a contribution to science at three levels: at the immediate level, it provides a basis for a computer program that seems likely to succeed in playing chess; at the middle level, game-playing programs help us to study and rationalize the processes of planning and decision-making; and, at the highest level, the study of the mind in action, as in the game of chess, leads to an understanding of human thought and of the human psyche.

Botvinnik does not say explicitly that his book is fundamental to the art and science of long-range planning. Nevertheless it is so, and Botvinnik correctly implies that it is. Each instance of the game of chess exemplifies in combat the interaction of planning and tactics. Botvinnik's concepts of the inexact problem, the variable horizon, and the setting of goals, are all close to the core of the problem of how to plan. Since chess provides a formalization of interpersonal conflict under a set of rules that is rich in possibilities, since the major games are recorded and fully available for study, and since the games do enlist the energies of many intelligent men, they provide us a microcosm in which the problems of planning can be studied in detail. The function of a long-range plan is to give guidance for present action; this is the same function that Botvinnik deals with, since the problem facing the chess player is the choice of a move to be made now, in the light of a general concept of the game.

I think the book itself is seminal. Like all seeds, it is compact, urgent, and cryptic. There is more in it than meets the eye at first reading. The title of the Russian version is *An Algorithm for Chess;* that is too narrow a description of its meaning and needs to be expanded. The audience should include not only chess players and computer theoreticians, but also students of management science, managers, psychologists, and the broad class of readers interested in the reach of the human mind. The title of this edition reaches the middle level of Botvinnik's contribution; within the next few years we should be seeing a book that reaches the highest level—when, as Botvinnik suggests, we can instill character into a computer program.

The urgency of the work is not in question. There is a wide body of literature to show that the principal scientific centers of the world recognize the need to study the playing of games as a means to further the understanding of the management of enterprises and the workings of the human mind. The formal study of games flowered in a major work by John von Neumann and Oskar Morgenstern in 1944. The formalization of chess via computer programs was begun by Claude Shannon, of the Bell Telephone Laboratories, in an address to the National Institute of Radio Engineers on March 9, 1949. (There were minor earlier efforts, but they dealt with very special situations; Shannon laid the major foundations for the use of the modern electronic computer, and all of its power, in the study of chess.) Shannon saw, as plausible extensions of chess-playing programs or of the theory underlying them, a set of programs for designing electronic circuits, a responsive switching system for a telephone net, and programs for carrying out many apparently intellectual functions, such as translating from one language to another, making simple military decisions, orchestrating melodies, and performing logical inferences.

Shannon's paper has been republished in at least two different collections; it should be read as an adjunct to Botvinnik's work. Also of interest is work by Allan Newell, J. S. Shaw, and Herbert Simon, and by Stanford University.

In mid-November of 1966 the Artificial Intelligence Laboratory of Project MAC at the Massachusetts Institute of Technology began the development of a chess-playing program. The product (by Greenblatt and Eastlake) won a Class D tournament trophy and has been made an honorary member of the United States Chess Federation and of the Massachusetts Chess Association, under the name of Mac Hack VI. It is said to be a better player than the Kotok-McCarthy program used by Stanford in the USA-USSR match that Botvinnik refers to in his first chapter.

Botvinnik discusses en passant the "inspiration" underlying the moves made by the chess master and dismisses the mystique as non-existent. Some relevant work is contained in a fundamental book by Adriaan de Groot, *Thought and Choice in Chess,* an account of a number of introspections by chess players facing the problem of making a move in a predetermined position. The psychoanalytic aspects of chess are discussed by Reuben Fine in *The Psychology of the Chess Player.*

I have said that the book is cryptic; I mean that for many members of the total potential audience, portions of the work and some of the references may be unfamiliar. Some explanatory material is appended in an effort to lessen such problems of unfamiliarity.

Appendix A is a translation of N. A. Krinitskii's preface to the Russian edition, which contains some mathematical calculations and some comments on the use of computers. Appendix B explains the chess notation used by Botvinnik, expands the calculations that Krinitskii makes in Appendix A, and touches on a number of subjects related to Botvinnik's main topic. For ready reference, Appendix C recapitulates the mathematical formulae developed by Botvinnik. Appendix D is an eclectic bibliography which offers a few pointers to the vast mass of published literature.

To the reader unfamiliar with chess literature, some of Botvinnik's remarks may seem overly astringent. The fact is that most chess authors are combat types and write with picturesque frankness. Botvinnik's style is very lively; I hope that I have conveyed something of its flavor.

Arthur Brown

Concord, Massachusetts
February, 1969

Preface
to the English Edition

Several months have gone by since *An Algorithm for Chess* was published in Moscow. This is not such a long time, but even now we can appraise the algorithm more precisely and make some general observations. This progress is largely due to the work done by V. Butenko on a program based on the algorithm.

An Algorithm is a hypothesis about the intuitive thought process of a chess master. Like any hypothesis, *An Algorithm* needs to be tested by experiment; in this case, an experimental test means writing a program and running it on a machine. This task has been taken on, at the Siberian Branch of the Academy of Sciences of the USSR, by a young mathematician and first-class chess player, V. Butenko.

There is a well-known method for solving a game, by analyzing the so-called mathematical tree of variations, which one builds up by scanning all the possibilities.

The method we are dealing with here has a specific feature: the variations-tree is analyzed after the path-tree is constructed. This method is more economical. The essence of it lies in the fact that in laying out the path-tree (with the aid of the code-tables listing the moves of the pieces) we need not scan in the usual sense. In a latent sense, the scanning does occur when we build the path-tree (in an open sense too, to some extent, when we use the code-tables to select paths that lie within the chosen horizon), since when we make up the code-tables we use the scan once and for all. Thus, when we make up the path-tree the scan is reduced to a minimum by using what might be termed the generalized experience of the past. When we begin to lay out the variations-tree we have already reduced the possibilities as far as we need to.

An Algorithm, as one might expect, turned out to be less than altogether exact and perfect. The reader should be warned of two essential pieces of imprecision: 1) in Formula (7) for computing the path-function of an attack path, and 2) concerning the static estimate of a position.

In deriving Formula (7) I omitted the possibility of a multiple exchange of pieces on a square common to two or more denial paths of order *n+1* and a denial path of order *n*. Since the latter path will not yet have been denied, the place-functions of these paths all have the value 1 except at the square that they have in common with the path of the last preceding denial. The place-function is evaluated at this square by reference to the exchanges that may go on there. After computing the functions for the last denial path, one must push on to the final goal—to compute the functions for the attack paths.

The formula for the static estimate of a position was not, strictly speaking, spelled out in the book, since the expectation Formula (9) cannot be used for this purpose. The expectation formula deals only with the advisability of further pursuit of a specific variation. A formula yielding a static estimate is needed, however, since at some point the scan of alternatives has to be given up (for instance, because of the principle that time must be properly used) and the position must be evaluated as is. Here the reader may join us in the field of action—the author, too, hopes to find such a formula.

Finally, I must admit to imprecision in formulating the mathematical map of a chess position. I said this map was to be constructed within the limits of a specified horizon. This is correct, but the statement needs refining.

Let us look at a well-known endgame by G. Nadareishvili. (White: Kh8, Pe3, g5, and h5. Black: Kf5, Bc2, Kte1, Pc5, e6. To win.) If White plays in a straightforward fashion, then after 1. g5-g6 Kf5-f6 2. g6-g7 Bc2-h7! 3. Kh8:h7 Kte1-f3! 4. g7-g8Q Ktf3-g5+ 5. Qg8:g5 (else Black gives perpetual check Ktg5-f7+-g5+) Kf6:g5 6. h5-h6 c5-c4 7. Kh7-g7 c4-c3 8. h6-h7 c3-c2 9. h7-h8Q c2-c1Q 10. Qh8-h6+ 11. Kg5-g4. Black is out of danger. Why? Because the White Pawn at e3 blocks the attack path of the White Queen at h6 against the Black Queen at c1. The White Pawn at e3 must be included in all the preceding mathematical maps. Of course, after the move 2... Bc2-h7 the White Pawn at e3 is in any case included in the 5-half-move horizon, but the variation 3. e3-e4 Kte1-f3 4. e4-e5+ Ktf3:e5 is rejected by the expectation Formula (9). The fact that the Pawn at e3 falls within the 5-half-move horizon has in principle no significance; even if it had fallen outside the horizon (after 2... Bc2-h7) it should nevertheless have been included in the mathematical map of the original position. Furthermore, although the variation 3. e3-e4 Kte1-f3 4. e4-e5+ Ktf3:e5 is rejected by the expectation Formula (9) in the mathematical map of the position after the move 4... Ktf3:e5, this variation itself is most useful from the point of view of the mathematical map of the final position. After 5. Kh8:h7 Kte5-f7(f3) 6. g7-g8Q Ktf7(f3)-g5+ 7. Qg8:g5+ Kf6:g5 8. h5-h6 c5-c4 9. Kh7-g7 c4-c3 10. h6-h7 c3-c2 11. h7-h8Q c2-c1Q 12. Qh8-h6+. Black loses the Queen.

Thus, if the scanning of the mathematical maps leads to the introduction of new pieces and squares, we must return to the initial map and insert those that appear in all other following maps. Then we must begin the scan all over again, and repeat the cycle until no more new squares or pieces appear.

The concept of the horizon is useful, but it must be applied with more subtlety than was suggested in *An Algorithm*. It is interesting to note that in my 1960 paper "People and Machines at the Chessboard" (Liudi i mašini za šakmatnoi doskoĭ), I set forth essentially this very method of focusing on the active pieces and squares, but in my work on *An Algorithm* I underestimated the importance of this idea.

The algorithm, and therefore the program, falls into three basic parts:

1. The knowledge of the rules of the game, that is, the ability to move pieces properly from one square to any other. This information is contained in the code-tables that were introduced in *An Algorithm*.

2. Forming the mathematical map of the position, the "sight of the board." One must see not the board with the pieces on it, but those pieces and squares that, together with the path-trees, are to be kept within the map. This is the way a master sees the board. In essence, this amounts to isolating the urgent information. For the programmer, this task is much harder than the first.

3. The ability to put a value on a position, both a static and a dynamic value, in the scanning process, by comparing the maps. This is perhaps the subtlest part of the algorithm, but it seems to me that the programmer must find it much more banal than the second part. Once the second part is finished, the programmer is through with the hardest part of the work. The third part will be difficult for the grandmaster, when he has to sharpen up the algorithm.

How does Butenko's work stand now?

He finished the first part quickly and without complications. He used only some 500 memory cells (of 45 binary digits per cell).

Then things came to a halt. As the proverb says, "skoro skazka skazivaets'a, da ne skoro delo delaets'a"—the word is quickly spoken, but the deed takes longer. In this case the word, i.e., the algorithm, was developed over the course of several years; but as yet the deed, i.e., the program, has taken scarcely two. The attempt to solve the second problem without laying down a general plan for the solution failed. In September of this year the first variant of the plan was completed; it was refined in October. The map of a single position takes up a little more than 2000 memory cells. I am convinced that Butenko is on the right track; he has begun to write this part of the program. Now is the critical period for all of the programming work.

As a chess player I see no way to solve the problem of choosing a move in a chess game but via the path sketched out in *An Algorithm*. I hope that this edition of *An Algorithm* will give new impetus to the testing of this hypothesis and will hasten the accomplishment of the tasks laid down by Shannon in 1950.

M. Botvinnik

Moscow
November, 1968

On the Computer Match: USSR-USA

While this book was in press, an event occurred that could not be ignored. This was the chess match between the computer at the Institute of Theoretical and Experimental Physics (ITEP) at Moscow and the computer at Stanford University (Palo Alto, California, USA), which ended in a 3 to 1 victory for Moscow. Before discussing it, I must make a few preliminary remarks about management systems.

In my opinion, every system for controlling events fulfills three functions quite distinct in principle: 1) it gets information; 2) it processes the information and makes a decision; and 3) it executes the decision.

This book, specialized as it may be, will nevertheless help to solve a problem of universal interest—the development of management systems and, in particular, the part of the system that processes information.

The tasks that every management (i.e., control) system has to perform fall into two classes. The first consists of those tasks in which the relevant volume of information can be completely processed by the system. Such tasks, or problems, can be dealt with precisely, and we shall call them *exact* tasks or *exact* problems.

The second class consists of those tasks in which the volume of information is so great that the system can process it only partially. Such tasks can be dealt with only partially, or inexactly, and we shall call them *inexact* tasks or *inexact* problems.

The same task may be exact or inexact, depending on the power of the control system confronting it, or, more precisely, on the power of the information-processing component of the control system.

In this book we consider an inexact problem—the game of chess. In 1950, when Claude Shannon proposed to "teach" a computer to play chess, he was, in essence, proposing to teach the computer to solve an inexact problem.

1

What is one to do when the volume of incoming information is too much, when it cannot be bitten off by the control system? There is nothing to do but cut it down to the point where it can be taken in and fully processed.

Shannon, at that time, proposed two principles on which an algorithm for playing chess could be founded:

1. Scan all the possibilities (moves) and construct a (so-called) tree with branches of equal length. In other words, all the variants of the moves to be inspected are computed to the same depth. When this depth is reached, the scan is discontinued. At the end of each variation (at the end of the branch) the position is evaluated by means of a numerical "weighting" function. By comparing the numerical values, one can choose the best move in any given starting position.

2. Not all possibilities are scanned; some are excluded from consideration by a special rule. The remainder are treated as in case 1. In this method, the depth of computation can clearly be greater.

The first principle is founded on the use of complete information within the limits of the specified depth of computation. Information of high value will be treated equally with information of low value. A substantial part of the work will be useless, and the principle is uneconomical. The quality of the solution will be below the capacity of the control system.

The second principle is better. If the rule for excluding weak moves is well founded, the processing of the information is more fruitful and the scan of alternatives is deeper. The second principle, even in this form, uses incomplete information. The branches of the tree are longer, even though they are all of the same length.

At the outset, we must acknowledge our debt to Shannon's insight. All computer programs for playing chess published by mathematicians in recent years are basically no different from those established in principle by Shannon.

At the same time, it must be said that in practice Shannon's recommendations seem not to be correct. For instance, according to Shannon, all the variations (branches of the tree) have the same length. It is obvious that if one had a rule for ending the study of a variation, some variations would be cut short early and others would be continued to greater length. An equal length of all branches must lead to a certain amount of unproductive work.

The use of the given weighting function to evaluate a position is also a doubtful procedure. Shannon proposed the inclusion of numerical "weights" for the material relation of forces, open lines, mobility of the pieces, advanced and doubled pawns, control of the center, and so on, which are all listed in every manual for beginners. We should note, as the authors of the textbooks usually do, that it is far from necessary to take account of all these factors at all times and that their calculation yields only a sketchy estimate of the position. To sum up, the mathematical goal of a chess game, according to Shannon, is a number—the value of the weighting function.

The four-game match played in 1966-67 between the programs at the ITEP in Moscow and Stanford University provided, in effect, a summary of the mathematical work that Shannon initiated in 1950. The Moscow program was based on Shannon's first principle, and the machine was of low power. The American program was based on Shannon's second principle, which is more perfected, and their machine was very powerful. And what happened? A fiasco for the Americans. The truth is that the first principle is easily implemented, but no one knew how to implement the second. The concrete realization of the second principle, by the American mathematician John McCarthy, turned out to be unsuccessful. The rule for rejecting moves was so constituted that the machine threw the baby out with the bath water.

Let us look at one of the games from the match.

Three Knights Opening

Moscow	Stanford

1. e2-e4 e7-e5 2. Ktg1-f3 Ktb8-c6 3. Ktb1-c3 Bf8-c5 (Handbooks on the openings usually give preference to the move 3. . . Ktf6. Then by a well-known combination White gains the initiative.) 4. Ktf3:e5 Ktc6:e5 (Weaker than 4. . . B:f2+ 5. K:f2 Kt:e5 6. d4.) 5. d2-d4 Bc5-d6 6. d4:e5 Bd6:e5 7. f2-f4 Be5:c3+ 8. b2:c3 Ktg8-f6 (An experienced chessplayer, of course, would never play with fire in this way and would have played 8. . . d6.) 9. e4-e5 Ktf6-e4.

Here White can advantageously continue with 10. Qd5 f5 (the only move) and then, possibly, 11. Ba3 d6 12. Bc4 Qe7 13. 0-0. The tactical subtlety lies in the fact that the continuation 10. . . Qh4+ 11. g3 Kt:g3 12. hg is harmless for White, since the Rook at h1 is protected by the Queen at d5. If 10. . . Kt:c3 11. Qc4 the Black Knight is denied a retreat path.

At the Moscow Central Chess Club I had an opportunity to hear a mathematician say why the machine did not play 10. Qd5 instead of 10. Qd3. It turns out that after 10. Qd5 Kt:c3 11. Qc4 Qh4+ 12. g3 the machine calculated the value of the weighting function and found it too low for a favorable evaluation of the move 10. Qd5. The depth of calculation was limited to five half-moves, and after 12. g3 the variation was broken off and the weighting function was calculated. At this point the machine turned out to be as blind as a bat. Since the Knight at c3 and the Queen at h4 lay quiet, and neither moved nor made noises, the machine in its blindness was unable to notice either Knight or Queen.

Then the mathematicians tried an experiment, which was successful: they increased the depth of calculation to seven half-moves. Then after 12. g3 the machine saw that the Knight and the Queen were simultaneously under attack, and the weighting function calculated after seven half-moves gave preference to the move 10. Qd5.

Alas! By the rules of the match, the program could not be altered, and the move 10. Qd5 was not made.

10. Qd1-d3 Kte4-c5 (10. . . . d5 suggests itself) 11. Qd3-d5 Ktc5-e6 (One gets the impression that the American program knows only one method of defense—to retreat. The necessary move would have been 11. . . . d6.) 12. f4-f5 Kte6-g5 (behold the pieces in a poor position) 13. h2-h4 f7-f6 14. h4:g5 f6:g5 15. Rh1:h7 Rh8-f8 16. Rh7:g7 c7-c6 17. Qd5-d6 Rf8:f5 18. Rg7-g8+ Rf5-f8 (else 18. . . . Kf7 19. Bc4x) 19. Qd6:f8x.

One's general impression is that McCarthy did not successfully implement Shannon's second method, whereas the Moscow mathematicians did successfully implement the first method. When the variations were connected with the annihilation of pieces, the weighting functions did well enough at determining an intelligent first move of the variation, but only when the variation had a logical end within the limits of five half-moves.

The reader will doubtless have formed the impression that the Moscow program was not too bad. The machine, perhaps, performed like a second-category player. True, there was a misunderstanding about the move 10. Qd5, but even masters have such mishaps.

To evaluate the Moscow program properly we must remember, first, that our knowledge is relative and the American machine played exceptionally badly, and second, that both the Moscow and Stanford programs are helpless in the endgame, so that the mathematicians agreed in advance that the games would be stopped after the 40th move. It is interesting to note that the endgame is precisely where the superiority of the master over the ordinary player becomes evident.

Is it impossible to implement Shannon's second method more successfully than McCarthy did? If the reader has enough patience, and will follow us to the end of the book, he will know the author's answer to this question.

The Algorithm as a Chess Player

Why a Machine is a Weak Player

Is there any need for a machine to play chess well? Opinions differ. Grandmasters, for example, become irritated at the question and say that this is idle talk—even if there is a need, the answer is far in the future, perhaps 50 years. Some scholars say that there is little use in wasting effort on "teaching" a machine genuine mastery of chess—to make it a second-rank player is enough. The importance and necessity of giving the machine a "higher education" will be proved later; for the present, the reader should accept them as proven.

The process of teaching a human to play chess falls into two stages. The first consists of assimilating the rules of the game, the moves, the value of the pieces, etc. The second consists in gaining mastery. Man successfully goes through both stages. The machine? There is a widespread belief that while the machine has passed the first stage long ago, it cannot take even a single step forward into the second.

What is the core of the matter? Why should a machine not be an excellent chess player? Is the task insoluble in principle? Is this the difference between man and machine?

No. The problem seems to be soluble. The difference between man and machine is not to be found here. The machine may play chess badly, like a beginning amateur, but the machine is not guilty. Man is guilty. He has not yet succeeded in teaching the machine, in transferring his experience to it.

What is involved in teaching a machine to play chess? There are two distinct possibilities: to write a finished program and give it to the machine, or to write a self-teaching program and give it to the machine. In both cases, the work must be done by a human. To write a finished program, one must master both chess and the art of programming. It is hard to say what will be needed for the writing

5

of a good program for learning chess. Aside from a knowledge of the rules, moves, and so on, a most likely requirement is for knowledge of the theory of self-teaching machines, and this up to now has been only barely sketched out. In this book we shall have in mind only the machine with the finished program (without self-teaching).

Thus, the machine needs a precisely-written program. Then it may turn out to be more capable than man; we know this from our experience in solving exact problems. Exact problems can be fully stated by means of mathematics, for example, in the form of equations. Algorithms for the solution of exact problems need only be translated into machine language and the deed is done; man has acquired a strong and untiring helper.

The situation is different with respect to those problems that I have conditionally called *inexact*, problems for which the mathematical methods have not been defined, so that there is nothing to translate into machine language. The inexact tasks include a wide range of possibilities. Man handles them more or less satisfactorily, but he does it subconsciously, so to speak, not knowing how he solves them. When man does not know his own method, nor any other, the machine is left without a program.

Turning the machine into a good aide in the solution of inexact problems (as powerful as in the solution of exact problems) can be done in one way only—by constructing a mathematically precise program for the solution of inexact problems, or, in the language of the mathematician, by formalizing the solution. This is where the problem lies.

It is a first-class problem. The range of inexact problems with a large number of possibilities covers tasks that are dealt with in many areas of human activity; they relate primarily to the sphere of command. It may well be true that the most important and difficult tasks of command are inexact.

Chess presents an inexact problem, with a large number of possibilities. Although the number of possibilities is large, it is theoretically finite; the finiteness, however, is irrelevant, since chess is played as though the number of possibilities were infinite. In practice, then, the problem of chess is like those important tasks just mentioned.

So far, the machine cannot perform these tasks, whereas man in his many centuries of history has accumulated a certain experience in the solution of inexact problems. But, frankly speaking, man himself is not overly successful in these areas. He solves such problems slowly and fitfully, for if in fact people solved inexact problems well, what need would we have of collective decisions? Who would think of collectively setting up or solving a system of equations? As a rule, that would be done by a single person. Likewise, collective decisions are not employed in calculating the trajectory of a space ship.

Collective solutions of inexact problems would be senseless if man were as powerful in this area as he is in dealing with exact problems. Even though the participants in a decision may not individually qualify for the task, there is nevertheless a chance for their joint success. If ten second-rate chessplayers, however, were to play a game in consultation, they might free themselves from gross oversights, but on the creative level would play a game corresponding to their abilities. For us, today, collective decisions are an absolute necessity. The collective process can and does promote the finding of one of the correct solutions to a problem.

For the solution of exact problems man has found an excellent assistant—the machine, when he has provided for it an exact program. This is, of course, a very good thing. But no less (and probably more) important would be the discovery of an assistant for the solution of inexact problems. We would have such an assistant if a precise program could be written for the machine. This can be done and will be done, not in 50 years, but much sooner.

Man solves inexact problems by relying on his accumulated experience and on intuition. The following method for creating an exact program for the solution of inexact tasks therefore suggests itself: *the program must be modelled on human thought processes.* In the sphere of chess, I pointed out this path in a lecture delivered at the Humboldt University in Berlin in 1960. It seems to me the only real way.

Here we may properly return to the question posed earlier: is a "higher education" needed for the machine in the game of chess? Yes, it is needed. The subtleties of a chess program can be understood only when the machine can play as strongly as a grandmaster, or, perhaps, even more strongly. The higher education is needed in order to model the algorithm used subconsciously by grandmasters. An attempt to set up a model of the algorithm used by second-class players, with the intent of transferring this algorithm to the programming of other inexact tasks, would probably mean only that these other tasks would be dealt with in a second-class fashion. If we want the computer to exceed man in the solution of inexact problems, and we try to bring this about by making use of our experience in creating programs for playing chess, then without doubt we shall succeed more quickly if our chess program enables the machine to beat a grandmaster.

The creation of a chess program promotes the creation of other more essential programs. But can we be sure that the principles on which the programs are constructed will be identical? Probably the answer is yes, but a certain amount of caution is needed: do all people think in the same way? Possibly some differences in the bases of the programs will be needed. Not everyone can be a grandmaster, just as some cannot be mathematicians or composers. And, of course, theoretically speaking, people in a single specialty may think differently.

Is it Necessary that the Machine Play Chess?

Before we begin work on our chess program, let us sharpen up our question about the usefulness of the task. There is no doubt that we need programs for the solution of inexact tasks with a large number of possibilities. But why should a chess program be the first step in this direction? Is chess complex enough to become the object of such an important investigation and experiment?

Chess does seem to be a good object. We have a great variety of forces (the pieces) engaged in battle. There are strong pieces and weak pieces. They have different ranges, and they move in different ways. One of the pieces (the Pawn) moves in a forward direction only but, what is most interesting, its line of motion differs from its line of attack. Thus a Pawn is easily blocked. Moreover, it can be converted into another piece. There is another special piece, the Knight. The Knight moves, not in a plane, but through space; this should not be forgotten by those inventors of all types of three-dimensional chess who criticize chess itself because of its "planarity." And then, the King, a remarkable piece indeed. Its value is infinite, so that one may not put it under attack. All the other pieces have value only in the presence of the King. The goal is checkmate, to win a piece of infinitely great value; the game ends when the King is lost. It is pertinent to note that chess is played according to precise rules. Sometimes the game ends without a winner, for instance if the only available moves would subject the King to attack (which is not permitted by the rules) and then—stalemate! Although the King is infinitely valuable, his attacking strength is not great; the King is probably no stronger than a Bishop or Knight. Once during the game a double move (castling) is allowed—yet another complication. Perhaps the reader is sufficiently persuaded? He probably knows to begin with that chess is a complex game. We may say, definitively, that modern chess is sufficiently complex for modern man.

In chess the moves are made one after the other. In other inexact tasks this may not be true, but it often is, and sometimes exclusively. Therefore this feature of chess cannot be the cause (or the occasion) for refusing to create a chess program.

The goal of chess—to win a piece of infinite value rather than all pieces—speaks in favor of programming chess, since in other important inexact problems one meets with infinitely valuable concepts.

Sometimes the chess player's thinking is surrounded by a mystic halo: the workings of the chess player's brain are represented as some miraculous, magical, altogether incomprehensible phenomenon. It is said, moreover, that not only is the thinking of chess "geniuses" mysterious, but even the gaining of advantage on the board is done by some magic laws of the art of chess. All this taken together announces itself as "creativity."

Certainly there is not one grain of logic in this. How a man (even a genius) can comprehend inexplicable laws of chess—and these laws are particularly inexplicable when they relate to combinational play—is indeed inconceivable. Why the thinking of the chess genius seems mysterious and miraculous, when the genius (as is discovered later) makes mistakes in a complex game nine times out of ten, and, while pondering his move, puffs away like a locomotive—this too is indeed inexplicable.

If we want to develop a chess program for a machine, we must decisively abandon all this rubbish of miracles, geniuses, incomprehensible laws, and other kinds of "creativity." We must assume that objective regularities, hitherto unknown, exist for chess combat, and that they can and must be known, together with the unknown modes of thought of the grandmaster. Moreover, we may assert that these regularities, and the mode of thought of the grandmaster, operate in children's chess, and not badly! Robert Fischer was champion of the USA at the age of fourteen: he encountered experienced and well-prepared masters, grown men. Samuel Reshevsky, as a child, gave adult exhibitions of simultaneous play, and very successfully (among others, a participant in one such session was the future world champion, M. Euwe, age nineteen).

Dear reader, only when we firmly decide, together, to reject all this mystical nonsense can we put the question: what, properly speaking, goes on in a chess game?

In my opinion, the process of playing chess (and probably any game) consists in a *generalized exchange.* By this term we mean an exchange in which (in the general case) the values traded may be tangible or positional ("invisible," situational). The goal of a generalized exchange is a relative gain of these tangible or positional (situational) values. There are not and cannot be other goals. In the end, this generalized exchange process in chess must lead to the winning of infinitely great tangible value (i.e., to mate).

The proof that something like this goes on in other games is outside our task. But we may remind ourselves that in a game as far from chess as soccer there is an exchange of tangible values (fatigue will change the effective strength of the player) and positional values (conjunctures). Independently of whether the player has the ball or not, he moves with respect to the ball, the goal posts, and other players so that the position of the team shall become more favorable. The objective, which ends the game if it is attained, is to win an infinitely large material value.

The tangible value of the pieces in chess is well known to all beginning chess players. But what of the invisible, conjunctural (positional) value of the pieces? This value depends on the position of the piece and on the role of the piece in the general combat then taking place on the board. The positional value of a piece is subject to sharp changes: the intangible value of a Pawn can be very great, for instance when it mates the enemy King.

We shall agree that when speaking of the chess algorithm that we are to construct we shall not mean those portions of it that contain the "knowledge" of the rules of the game, the moves, the material value of the pieces, and the goal of the game. We shall assume, moreover, that the algorithm imitates the mode of play of the human, that is, it defines a scan and an evaluation of the available moves. The scan, however, is controlled, since a complete scan is in practice impossible because of the very great number of moves.

What must the algorithm now envisage?

As a minimum, it must envisage a solution to the following three problems:

1. How to limit the number of alternatives? Clearly, if the number of alternatives is very great, the task is beyond the strength of man (and of the machine, too). Therefore the algorithm must lead to the exclusion of senseless moves. In calculating the variations, it must take into account only moves that make sense. In this case, the number of possibilities will be reduced, and the task becomes real.

2. When to stop computing a variation? This requirement is also self-evident. Man uses certain rules to decide when the analysis of a variation can and should be stopped; that is, man has a criterion for evaluating a variation. Such a precise criterion should be given to the machine. Then the machine (and the man) will be able to evaluate a variation and reject those that have no meaning. This also lightens the work, like the rejection of senseless moves.

3. What move to make if the analysis of variations gives no clear answer? This question is important. In fact, when the analysis of variations leads to no definite result, the grandmaster chooses his move on the basis of special considerations. The machine, under these circumstances, must be given a clear-cut prescription.

The solution of these three problems is essential, even though we may later find that it is not sufficient.

A Mathematical
Representation of Chess

The Primacy of the Attack: Assertion and Negation

The algorithm that we are to work with rests on two principles. The first is that both sides in the end have to strive for material gain (this is not in the rules of the game, but is true in practice). It follows that everything begins with the attack, and the attack defines the trajectory (the path) of the attacking piece. A chess game may be thought of as a debate between the two sides; the attack is an assertion, the defense a negation. The assertion can bring forth a negation, which defines the path of defense (the negation).

Can there be a defense (a negation) without an attack (an assertion)? Probably not. True, it seems to be generally felt that a piece can "protect" another even in the absence of an attack. For example, in Fig. 1, the King at b2 "protects" the Queen at a2. In this position, according to the rules of the game, Black may not attack the White Queen, so this is all merely a combination of words. The King at b2 is in fact not defending the Queen at a2, since there is no attack on the Queen and there cannot be one.

We may negate not only an assertion but also a negation; that is, we may not only defend (if there is an attack) but we may also hinder a defense.

The Scope of the Task

The second principle amounts to saying that we must find an approximate solution by limiting the problem. If we are to consider all possible attacks, the problem becomes impossibly difficult to solve. We have to limit the problem and look at only a few attacks and the corresponding negations. In other words, we must establish a *horizon* and deal with only those attacks that fall within it. Within the limits of the horizon the problem will be (or should be) solved exactly.

Fig. 1. Can the White Queen be attacked?

Fig. 2. Whose move?

Time and Material in Chess: The Elementary Mathematical Functions

The mathematical model of chess is founded on very simple functions which reflect only two factors. Because material gain is the basis of chess play, the first factor is the tangible value of the pieces, which amounts to their average strength (except for the King, whose value is infinite and whose strength is small, and for the Pawn in certain cases where he can become a Queen). The second factor is the time needed to move the interacting pieces, that is, the number of half-moves needed to get the pieces from one specified square to another.

It is worthwhile to agree on the way in which time is to be measured in chess. Normally, in the textbooks, it is measured in moves. But this is hardly suitable. In Fig. 2 we might imagine that both the White Rook at d1 and the Black Bishop at b6 attack the square d4. Both pieces can occupy it in one move, but the situation is wholly ambiguous, since everything depends on knowing whose move it is. If we measure chess time in half-moves, the ambiguity disappears. If we know, in the case in question, that the White Rook at d1 can occupy the square at d4 in two half-moves (or that the Black Bishop can occupy it in one half-move) everything becomes clear—Black is to move. So that is the right way; one must measure the time taken to move from one square to another. But when a piece is standing still (while the enemy moves), does time pass? Standstill time must be counted too, and the time for movement is the sum of the half-moves of standstill and the half-moves of motion. Chess time is to be measured in *half-moves,* not moves.

In the opening, to play 1. e4, White needs one half-move and to play 1. . . e5 Black needs two half-moves.

For all of our calculations connected with tangible values we shall use Shannon's price-list: K=200, Q=9, R=5, B and Kt=3, P=1. We shall sometimes use only the symbols for the piece, and at other times supply the coordinates of a square, for instance Kg5.

The speed and the transit time of a piece are determined by the rules of chess.

The Intangible Value of the Attack

An attacking piece has an intangible value or values in addition to its tangible value; its total value is the sum of the tangible and intangible values. The intangible value of an attacking piece reflects its ability to annihilate an enemy piece. The *condition of capture* consists in the fact that at the moment of capture the intangible value of the attacking piece is equal to, and of opposite sign from, the tangible value of the captured piece. The algebraic sum of the two values is equal to zero, and on the square where the capture takes place there is left only the tangible value of the capturing piece (neglecting other possible intangible values of that piece). This is our mathematical model of capture.

Until the capture, the intangible value is zero (although this "zero" has a number of shades of meaning). At the moment of capture it becomes suddenly different from zero, with a jump, and stays frozen at its new level until the end of the game.

One and the same piece may join in different actions. It may simultaneously assert (attack an enemy piece), negate (defend a piece of its own side), or negate a negation (support an attack by an ally), and so on.

The Path of a Piece

An attack must have real features. There must be an object of attack and a path, made up of actual squares, over which the attack is to be carried out. These squares are of two types: 1) squares where the pieces come to rest, which we shall denote by α, and 2) squares over which the pieces pass, denoted by β. There must always be α-squares; there need not be β-squares. When the King, the Knight or the Pawn makes a move (except for castling and the initial two-square move of the Pawn) there are no β-squares. Similarly, there are none when the Queen, Rook or Bishop moves to an adjacent square.

The Three Types of Defense

The defense (the negation) is connected first of all with the capture of an attacking piece; the control of an α-square is always linked to an attack from ambush. A defense may be realized by blockade, that is, by occupying an α-square (if a β-square is blockaded it automatically becomes an α-square). And, finally, a defense may be made by retiring the piece that is under attack.

The Mathematical Differentiation of the Two Sides

One must distinguish the sides mathematically, rather than by color. Let us agree to denote the tangible values of the White pieces by real numbers and of the Black pieces by imaginary numbers. This is convenient, since the intangible value of an attacking piece should not be confounded with its tangible value. On the other hand, the intangible value of an attacking piece should be of the same nature as the tangible value of its victim. This notion makes possible the mathematical representation of the attack.

The total value of the White King, attacking a Black Knight, will then be[1] $K-jKt·\psi·J$, and the total value of the Black Queen attacking a White Rook is $jQ-R·\psi·F$, where ψ, Θ, and F are functions to be defined in a later section.

We will denote the tangible value of a White piece by M, and of a Black piece by N. The total value of an attacking piece will be expressed by the complex number $M - \Sigma(jN·\psi·\Theta)$ for White and $jN - \Sigma(M·\psi·F)$ for Black.

---

[1] The path function F will be used for an attacking White piece, and Θ will refer to the Black pieces. The symbol j means $\sqrt{-1}$.

Functions of the α-squares and Attack Paths

A piece under attack can be captured when two factors coincide: 1) all the α-squares on the attack path (including the initial position of the attacking piece and the square containing the piece under attack) are free and clear of danger, and 2) all the α-squares to which the attacked piece may retreat are either held or are dangerous. This is the necessary condition for a capture.

Let us agree that to every α-square of a path there corresponds a function f. When the α-squares of the path are free and secure, $f=1$; otherwise, $f=0$. The symbol f_i denotes the function f corresponding to the i-th α-square.

The function ψ, mentioned a moment ago, is defined as being equal to zero when the attacker has not yet reached the α-square where its victim waits; when the attacking piece has reached the square containing the stricken piece, the value of ψ becomes 1.

Taking into account the total value of a piece, the definition of the function f, and the conditions of capture, we see that the expression

$$F = \Pi \, (1 - f_k) \cdot \Pi f_i \tag{1}$$

(where the f_k are the place-functions of the retreat-paths and Πf_i is the product of the place-functions of the attack-paths) has the value 1 if all the $f_k=0$ and all the $f_i=1$, that is, if the attack is ineluctable. Otherwise the value of F is zero.

The functions f and ψ were defined verbally; the function F was defined by means of the symbolic Formula (1). It is not too hard to find a mathematical definition of f and ψ.

Let us write down a formula for the function ψ. It is easy to see that the expression

$$\psi = \frac{1}{2} \cdot \left(1 - \frac{2n_{ir} - 1}{|\, 2n_{ir} - 1\,|}\right) \tag{$2)^2$}$$

meets the requirements placed on the function by its verbal definition. Here i denotes the square on which the attacking piece rests, r denotes the square on which the intended victim rests, and n_{ir} is the number of half-moves needed for the attacking piece to go from the α-square i to the α-square r. The function ψ is zero unless $n_{ir}=n_{rr}=0$, that is, unless the capture has taken place; then $\psi=1$.

Let us now write down an expression for the function f. We recall that when the α-squares of a path are blocked by pieces of the same color, $f=0$. This corresponds to the rules of the game and will therefore not be taken into account in making up the formula for f.

We first write down a formula describing the possibility of controlling or blockading the α-squares of the path:

$$\rho_n = \frac{1}{2} \cdot \left(1 - \frac{n_{ik} - n_{rk} + a}{|\, n_{ik} - n_{rk} + a\,|}\right) \tag{3'}$$

---

[2] The absolute value of the quantities $2\,n_{ir} - 1$ is always positive.

Here n_{ik} is the number of half-moves needed for the piece at the α-square i to go to the α-square k of the trajectory, and n_{rk} is the number of half-moves needed for the piece controlling (or blockading) the α-square k to get there from the α-square r. For control, $a=2$; for blockade, $a=0$. It is not hard to prove that if the square k can be controlled or blockaded, $\rho_n=0$; otherwise, $\rho_n=1$.

Even when controlled, however, an α-square may be safe provided the occupation of the square does not entail material loss, i.e., if the function

$$\tau_m = \frac{1}{2} \cdot \left(1 + \frac{m + 0.1}{|m + 0.1|}\right) \tag{3''}$$

(where m is a measure of material gain) is equal to 1. The loss of material, for the purposes of this formula, is taken as a negative gain. We may now write down the formula for the function f:

$$f = \tau_m + \rho_n - \tau_m \cdot \rho_n \tag{3}$$

Fig. 3. Attack the King and win the Queen.

If material loss is not foreseeable on an α-square, or if the square is not controlled, it is safe, and Formula (3) yields a value of 1 for the place-function.

Here we must make a most important remark. Let us look at Fig. 3; if the move is White's, one of the two intangible values of the White Rook (for a three-half-move computation) is given by $-jKg5\cdot0(3)\cdot1(e1)\cdot1(e5)\cdot1(g5)\cdot(1-0)$, that is, $-jKg5\cdot0\cdot1\cdot1\cdot1\cdot1^3$.

---

[3] We take it that $\psi = 0\,(3)$; this means that $\psi = 0$, and the minimum number of half-moves needed to convert ψ to the value 1 is 3. The expression $1(e5)$ means that the function f has the value 1 at the square e5. More detail on this point will be given later.

The attack on the King being irresistible, is mate unavoidable? Not at all; Black has a defense! The "1's" making up this intangible value refer only to the security of the path, to the fact that the local skirmishes on the α-squares of the attack paths will be resolved in favor of the attacking side. But the side under attack must choose correctly—since it loses the local war on all the α-squares—which of these skirmishes it will lose. Obviously, the chosen square should be the one that entails the smallest loss. In this case, of the seven α-squares where such skirmishes are possible (e5, f5, f4, g4, g5, h4, h5), the smallest loss occurs at e5 and f5 (the latter if the Queen blocks the check) where Black loses 4 units of material (Q—R), while on the other squares f4, g4, g5, h4, and h5, Black loses nearly 200 units (K—R).

Thus, when the gain of material on the intermediate α-squares of a path (the function F of the path being equal to 1) is less likely than the gain of material on the final square, the object of the attack is changed. The material value of the attack is decreased and becomes the value of the least possible win on any of the α-squares of the attack path.

Let us agree to denote the possible gain on the final square of an attack-path by m_k and the minimum value of the gain on any intermediate α-square i of the same path by m_i. We introduce the functions

$$\tau_{\Delta m} = \frac{1}{2} \cdot \left(1 + \frac{m_i - m_k + 0.1}{|m_i - m_k + 0.1|} \right) \tag{4'}$$

$$\varphi = 1 - \rho_n - \tau_{\Delta m} + \rho_n \cdot \tau_{\Delta m} \tag{4''}$$

where we write $\Delta m = m_i - m_k$ and ρ_n is the function already defined in (3'). Then the tangible value attacked will be

$$m = m_k \cdot \psi_k + \Delta(m, \psi) \cdot \varphi_i \tag{4}$$

where

$$\Delta(m), \psi = m_i \cdot \psi - m_k \cdot \psi_k.$$

If $m_i < m_k$, then $\Delta_m = 0$. But then, since $\rho_n = 0$ (the square α_i is controlled), $\psi = 1$, and by Formula (4) the tangible value under attack is diminished. If the square α_i is not controlled, $\rho_n = 1$, $\psi = 0$, and the square has no effect on the magnitude of the value under attack.

The path-function suffers no change, since all these changes of the value under attack take place if $F = 1$; the α-squares on the path are not changed by a change in the value under attack, even though for the gain of material a shorter path may be required.

The "Hop-Skip" Rule

This rule facilitates the calculation of ψ and ρ_n, which change their values with every half-move; it is founded on the fact that half-moves take place in turn.

Suppose we agree that a piece on square i can be moved to square k in n half-moves. Let a half-move be made, in regular turn, but not of the piece in question—let another piece of the same color be moved. Then the rule says: if the path from i to k has not changed, the number of half-moves needed will be *n+1* in place of *n*. It is now the opposing side's turn; if after the opposing half-move nothing has happened to the path, the number of half-moves needed returns to the value n.

The Intangible Values of the Negation

To analyze the mathematical map it is necessary to know the values of the negation, and we may now write down the corresponding formulae.

The intangible values of the attack are based on capture; the intangible values of the negation are based on a change of the values being negated. These changing values may be either the value of a path-function or the tangible value of an object under attack.

The intangible value of a first-order denial of a place-function belonging to an attack path is

$$0_1 = - M_0 \cdot \psi_0 \cdot \Delta_i F_0 \cdot \psi_{1i} \cdot F_{1i} \tag{5}$$

and the value of a second-order denial (negation of the negation) of the place-function at the square α_k of a negation-path is

$$0_2 = - M_0 \cdot \psi_0 \cdot \Delta_i F_0 \cdot \psi_{1i} \cdot \Delta_k F_{1i} \cdot \psi_{2k} \cdot F_{2k}. \tag{6}$$

Here M_0 is the tangible value of the pieces under attack, and

$$\Delta_i F_0 = F_0 - \frac{F_0}{f_{0i}} f'_{0i}$$

is the value of the place function which is being negated and f'_{0i} is the new value of the function after the negation has been taken into account[4]) and, finally, F_{1i} is the path-function of the first-order negation, etc.

In the Formulae (5) and (6) we take account only of changes in the path-function; we do not take account of changes in M_0 that might arise from changes in the place-functions of the α-squares—[see Formula (4)].

Calculation of the Function F for an Attack Path

We may calculate the function F as follows: first, we assume that the place-functions are such that $F=1$; then we compute all first-order negations and make the necessary corrections; finally, we compute second-order negations, make the corrections, and go on to higher orders. Mathematically, the function F_0^R of a real attack path will be

---

[4]The division process in the fraction F_0/f_{0i} is carried out only formally, pending substitution of the values for the f_{0i}.

$$F_0^R = \prod_{i=1}^{h}(1-f) \cdot \prod_{h=1}^{q} \left\{ f_{0i} + \Delta f_{0i} \cdot \prod_{h=1}^{q} \left\{ f_{1k} + \Delta f_{1k} \right. \right.$$

$$\times \prod_{m=1}^{p} [f_{2m} + \Delta f_{2m} \cdot \prod_{n=1}^{r} (f_{3n} + \Delta f_{3n} \cdot \prod_{1}^{s} \cdots \left. \right\} \qquad (7)[5]$$

where $\Delta f_{0i} = f_{0i}^R - f_{0i}$, etc.

When $\prod_{1}^{s}$, $\prod_{n=1}^{r}$, $\prod_{m=1}^{p}$ and $\prod_{k=1}^{q}$ are equal to unity, then $f_{0i}=1$ is denied, and $f_{0i}=f'_{0i}$.
If however $\prod_{k-1}^{q} = 0$, we have $f_a = f'_{0i} = 1$.

On a retreat path, which is reflected by the function $(1-f)$, the calculation of the real path is the same as for $\prod f_i$. This is not taken into account in the Formula (7). The method of calculation will become clear after we take up an experiment that will be described later.

Calculation of the Function τ_m

To calculate the function τ_m [Formula (3″)], we must calculate the quantity m—the material balance resulting from an exchange on an α-square. When one or two pieces are exchanged, the problem is simple; when there is a possibility of multiple exchange, it is useful to have a formula to facilitate the calculations

$$\Sigma|jN| - \Sigma|M| \geqslant -|jN|\cdot\theta \qquad (8')$$

$$\Sigma|jN| - \Sigma|M| \leqslant |M|\cdot F \qquad (8'')$$

The first formula defines the possibility for White of continuing the exchange; the right hand side of the inequality represents the tangible value of the Black pieces that are subject to capture. The left side represents the value of the pieces already exchanged. When the inequality is reversed, the exchange should be broken off.

The second, and similar, formula represents Black's view of the variation. When the inequality is reserved, it is unfavorable for Black. The tangible value of the pieces yet to be captured must not be less than the relative material losses.

The General Exchange Formula

When a move or a sequence of moves is completed, there may have been an exchange of total, tangible, or intangible values. We must understand "exchange" in the generalized sense, as a change in values.

Data on the exchange potentials of the whole board are collected as a whole

---

[5] The indices *h, q, p, r* and *s* denote the number of factors in the corresponding products $\prod$. See also the author's preface.

and then the evaluation of variations is carried out, i.e., the scanning of the moves that make sense. One has to keep in mind the fact that a variation made up of sensible moves may in fact be senseless.

The study of a variation (the scan of the moves) should go on as long as hope remains of recouping one's losses. Therefore

$$\Sigma\,|\,jN\,|-\Sigma\,|\,M\,|\geqslant-\Sigma\,|\,jN\,|\cdot\theta-\Sigma\,(1-\theta)\cdot|\,jN\,|\cdot\gamma \qquad (9')$$

where

$$\gamma=\frac{1}{2}\cdot\left(1-\frac{\Delta q+0.1}{|\,\Delta q+0.1\,|}\right) \qquad (10)$$

is the function defining the change in the number q (the number of α-squares where $f{=}0$) in the half-move under study; $\gamma{=}{+}1$ if q decreases, and $\gamma{=}{-}1$ otherwise.

If the inequality $(9')$ holds good, White should continue his study of the variation. The left-hand side of the inequality counts up the relative material losses for White; the first term on the right measures the winnings if the doomed pieces are destroyed ($\theta = 1$). We should note that the material destined for destruction is to be computed via Formula (4). The second term on the right side of the inequality deals with the tangible values not yet available for destruction ($\theta = 0$) but not out of the reach of destiny provided the scan is extended, since the function $\gamma{=}{+}1$ changes to the favorable side, and here the count of the values that we can hope to capture is to be computed while disregarding Formula (4).

The like formula for Black is

$$\Sigma\,|\,jN\,|-\Sigma\,|\,M\,|\leqslant\Sigma\,|\,M\,|\cdot F+\Sigma\,(1-F)\cdot|\,M\,|\cdot\gamma \qquad (9'')$$

The mathematical representation of chess is a set of shifting total values; both sides try to change this set of values in accordance with the Formulae $(9')$ and $(9'')$, which we shall call the *expectation formulae*.

The Horizon (The Limitation of the Task)

We said earlier that we would consider some attacks only, not all, and the negations connected with them.

Suppose we think of a simile—I hope that chess players will not be insulted. How can a dog count her litter? She has to know how to count: if "counting" were not included in her "algorithm" she would never notice a disappearance of her offspring. But even if the method were at hand, without some limitation of the task she could never keep up with the count: her canine capabilities would not be equal to an infinite litter-count (say, a dozen puppies). She counts at a very low level: one, two, three, and "many." The disappearance of one puppy out of five would not be noticed! But for the preservation of the canine race the ability she has is sufficient.

We must define this notion of "many" for chess. Then we shall have to calculate only a limited number of functions and the task becomes real.

In any given position, the more the number of half-moves that we have to make to get an attacking piece to the square where the enemy waits, the more complex the problem, and vice versa. The longer the path, i.e., the greater the number of squares to be stopped on, the more complex the battle becomes. Thus, the conclusion comes to us of its own accord—to limit the problem by inspecting only those pieces that can reach an enemy-held square in no more than a specified number of half-moves h (on a board free of obstacles, clear of other pieces).

This condition for the inclusion of a piece inside the horizon is necessary but not sufficient. We must not overlook the possibility of converting a β-square into an α-square through the presence of obstacles, pieces blocking an attack path. Then the number of half-moves will increase by at least two for each blocked β-square. Moreover, when an α-square contains a piece of the same color as the attacker, the number of half-moves increases also by at least two. This increase may throw the path beyond the horizon.

An attack falling within the horizon is included in the mathematical calculations—otherwise, it is not. The horizon is the boundary of the region containing those pieces, and only those pieces, that can take an active role within the given limits of time for movement. (See the remarks on this point in the author's preface.) We construct a mathematical map and carry through the analysis of it for attacks that can be consummated in one half-move, then we go on to two half-moves, and so on. We carry the analysis to the point where our resources fail, unless we succeed at an earlier time.

When the position is complex (open) there are many attacks, and the horizon lies nearby. In the endgame, where there are fewer attacks, the game takes on a more nearly "forced" character and the horizon recedes. The maximal horizon is defined by the capabilities of the apparatus at work within the player, whether the player be man or machine.

A simile may help to clarify this notion of the horizon and its determinants. Let us suppose that a parachute-jumper has come down in a bog and wants to get onto solid ground. The bog is wide; its edges are hundreds of yards away. How does our hero proceed, if he cannot find a clear path from where he is to where he wants to be? He cannot take in the whole plot at one coup and pick out the entire path . . . he must act soon . . . darkness is falling!

In all probability he will inspect the bog in some given direction for the first five to ten yards, choose a path from hummock to hummock, as safe a path as he can find, and take the first step. He will make the next step after a similar preparation. Our hero again inspects the five- to ten-yard horizon. It will have already changed because of his action. He accepts the solution to the second-step problem, and so on until he clears the bog.

We could prove that all the devices used in chess war—attack (from both sides), blockade (by either side), and (mutual) retreat—can all be accounted for in an initial mathematical map constructed on an attack contained within four half-moves.

Play for Annihilation

In constructing the mathematical map for a given horizon (a map based on the intangible values of the attack) and in analyzing the changes in the map resulting from the several variations of the moves that are scanned, Formula (9) allows us to compute only the tangible changes. At the moment, we are speaking only of immediate attack and capture, and we refer to *play for annihilation*.

This, however, is only one side of the question. If the horizon were unlimited, annihilation would decide the entire game. But the horizon is not unlimited, and therefore another side of the problem develops. What do we do if the forcing of the game to annihilation comes up with no clear answer? Or if it gives an answer, but the answer is doubtful because the horizon is limited? We need another criterion, which may help us to stay away from gross blunders that we might make because the horizon is limited and may help us to find additional meaningful moves.

Play for Change of the Functions

This additional criterion ought not to raise any new complex problems, that is, it should keep us within the horizon (although the horizon is now "positional" it should be no different from the former horizon). But a new situation appears. Almost all negation paths are shorter than the set limits, and they do not reach the horizon. This happens partly because some attack paths are short, but not entirely for this reason, since even for longer attack paths lying at the limit [see Formula (7)] the negation path may be shortened to the vanishing point by being related to squares close to, or at, the attacking piece. This "unused" horizon is a reserve that should be cashed in.

Let us go back to our parachute-jumper. To get away from his landing-point, he has to do something at once to get out of danger. He chooses his equipment, he looks about; is there a log or a board? He tries to find some way to assure the safety of his exit path.

The chessplayer does this too. If the attack path is unsafe (closed) the master (like the parachute-jumper) looks about him: can he bring other pieces into the game, to better the attack paths (the functions) against the enemy pieces and lessen the attacks against his own pieces? This is what "positional" play amounts to.

I believe that this part of the theory (on positional warfare) is radically different from what has been presented up to now. And here is where the master differs in his play from the weakling.

For a negation path the quantity ψ_{1i} [see Formula (5)] is defined by Formula

(2). Here the value of n_{ir} corresponds to the value of n_{rk} in Formula (3'). If n_{rk} has a value such that $\rho_n=0$, the negating piece falls into the mathematical model of play for annihilation. If $\rho_n=1$, we know that n_{ir} is large enough so that the negating piece is out of the game. But can the negating piece still take part in the combat?

We broaden the set of negating pieces under consideration by including those one half-move further away, compared to the number of half-moves required to take part in play for annihilation. We have the right to do this until we reach the horizon. Then we shall collect information on the pieces that are not now active but might in the future enter a play for annihilation! They will enter, in general, not by making the capture directly, but by changing an attack path in a favorable direction. Positional play takes on decisive significance when functions f_i of α-squares with value zero predominate on an attack path.

It may happen that for economy of force we ought not to consider an attack on all the α-squares of the attack and negation paths. We may impose a restriction, for instance, by considering those place-functions having the value zero. If q be taken as the number of α-squares in the trajectory at which $f=0$, and the condition

$$q < \nu \tag{11}$$

is satisfied (where ν is the number given as limiting the complexity of the task being solved), then we should consider the participation of other pieces in the attack on those α-squares. Play directed at changing a path has the same character, and proceeds by the same formulae, as play for annihilation, with the distinction that now the object of the attack is not an enemy piece itself, but a change in the attack-functions. We evaluate positional play by Formula (11).

If what we have said has some relation to the truth, we may conclude that the positional estimate made by a master tends to be rather primitive. One possibility for improvement that comes to mind is the use of modern mathematical methods to define moves most likely to lead to success. Then to every "positional" move there would correspond a weighting function (a number) which would allow the definition of the most useful move, by a more perfect method than the chess master now uses.

The "style" of a chess player is founded on position play. All masters use the same method in forced play for annihilation. In positional play there is a choice: one may increase the number q in the attack paths of the other side, without attending to one's own functions $f=0$ (this is the passive style), or one may decrease the number q in one's own attack paths and decrease it also in the enemy's (this is the active, or sharp style). There are other possibilities.

Types of Value

A method for classifying the values of pieces is extremely useful in evaluating a position. We shall classify them by the nearness of the pieces to annihilation (removal from the board).

In the first type of value we include pieces removed from the board. At first impression this seems senseless, but the first impression is wrong. Pieces knocked out of the game "take part" in it; the balance of the annihilated pieces (the balance of their tangible values) contributes to the estimate of the position.

The second type refers to pieces that are subject to certain capture during a play for annihilation, that is, the path functions F and Θ have the value 1 at these pieces. In defining these functions we take into account only those pieces that have entered the mathematical map of a play for annihilation.

The third type of value is formally defined in the same way as the second, with the difference that the function [Formula $(3'')$] is evaluated by taking into account not only the pieces entering the mathematical map of a play for annihilation, but also those entering the "positional" play and falling within the positional horizon. The functions of negation paths are equal to 1 in this connection, so that we may certainly expect that after the pieces falling within the positional horizon have been moved, the functions of the attack paths will also equal 1.

The fourth type of value consists of those corresponding to path functions (attack and negation) different from 1; there is no reason to suppose that in the immediate future the values of these pieces will change.

I believe that behind this formal classification scheme lies a well-known concept. For instance, in evaluating a combination the root is the need to test whether it is possible to make up losses in Type I values by converting Type II values into Type I. This is how one analyzes the map.

The so-called, and well-known, *positional sacrifice* is possible only when there is a chance that Type I losses can be compensated *in the future* (but not at the end of the scan of the half-moves) by Type III values, through conversion of these values during the course of the game to Type II, and then to Type I.

Positional play consists in converting Type IV values to Type III (and the reverse).

The Position Estimate

The direction of the inequality sign as given below

$$\Sigma \mid jN \mid - \Sigma \mid M \mid \geqslant \Sigma \mid M \mid \cdot F - \Sigma \mid jN \mid \cdot \theta \qquad (12)$$

indicates that White may not be at a disadvantage if he makes a positional sacrifice; when the sign is reversed, the position favors Black.

All the symbols are as given in Formula (9). We need only remember that the functions F and Θ are calculated using the positional horizon. Positional warfare is evaluated by Formula (11).

Ending the Study of the Map

We said earlier that the study of the map should be continued as long as directed by the expectation Formulae (9′) and (9″). If no pieces on the map fall within the positional horizon, we do not know what to do. But the use of the positional horizon allows the analysis to be broken off at an arbitrary moment, with the aid of Formulae (11) and (12).

This is most important. We can combine a deep calculation for a close horizon with a shallow calculation for a distant horizon, and then choose our move.

This part of the theory, touching on positional play, should not be thought of as finished; it must be refined by the necessary experiments, which must be done for the whole theory as well.

The Technique of Constructing the Map

Failures of the Mathematicians

The reader is now familiar with the principles involved in constructing and analyzing a mathematical map of a chess position. I believe that the chess algorithm presented in this book and based on these principles represents the thought processes of a chess master during the game. The master knows the rules of the game; he knows how to move the pieces from one square to another and so has never raised the question of constructing a formalized algorithm for moving the pieces. But as soon as we need to translate the logical algorithm of a chess master into machine language, we have to teach the machine the rules and the process of moving. We must program the rules for moving the pieces, since the machine does not know how to play.

The reader may here press a claim against the author: is not the question stood on its head? Would it not have been better to construct the algorithm for the rules of the game and the moves of the pieces at the outset, and only then proceed to the logical algorithm? In other words, should not the positions of this and the previous chapter be reversed? No. It would not have been better to do so! Everything has been done properly. We assumed at the outset that the rules of the game were already known (including the rules for moving the pieces) and then we constructed the logical algorithm. The algorithm for the rules did, as it were, precede the logical algorithm. But to construct the formal algorithm for moving the pieces and prepare it for the machine before constructing the logical algorithm would be a most doubtful enterprise.

Practice is the test of truth. In the last twenty years many mathematicians have "educated" the machine in the game of chess. As I understand it, they began by teaching the machine the rules of the game and then considered the logical algorithm; the process of writing a chess program began with the programming of the moves and then, only then, passed on to the preparation of a program to implement a method of play. The results were weak. I shall be bold enough to say that the weakness of these results can be explained by the fact that first the mathematicians programmed the moves of the pieces and only then programmed the logic. The program for moving the pieces was conceived as a program for making single moves. No method was devised for moving pieces to an arbitrarily selected square. It was tacitly assumed that such a method would be equivalent to a complete scan of the possible chess positions and would therefore be impossible in practice.

When the mathematicians turned their attention to the logical parts of the program, their policy had already been frozen. If the machine "knows" only how to move pieces in a single move, the mathematical map for a horizon of more than two half-moves becomes very difficult. An exception was made for the King. The machine knew how to announce *check* (an attack consisting of no more than four half-moves). Sometimes the machine was taught to announce *guard*, an attack on the Queen (also possible in four half-moves.) But as a rule, the mathematical map was constructed with a horizon no deeper than two half-moves. The machine horizon was the horizon of a beginning chessplayer.

Therefore, in the discussions at the Central Chess Club (May 13, 1966) on the mathematical representation of chess, the mathematicians criticizing the logical algorithm presented in the preceding chapter singled out as a deficiency the necessity for moving pieces from one square to an arbitrarily chosen other square, since the machine was not capable of doing this. Alas, this is testimony not to the weakness of the algorithm submitted for judgment, but only to the fact that the machine program for moving the pieces was unsatisfactory.

The author has been lucky enough to avoid the common fate only because he did not connect his work with machine programming until the principles of the logical algorithm had been laid down.

How a Man is Taught

Skeptics, to be sure, may say that man too learns the rules for moving pieces in one move only and they may ask how a man can have a map with a horizon greater than two half-moves. How does his process differ from that of a computer?

The differences are essential. Man uses subconscious algorithms which let him rework the rule for making single moves into a rule for moving pieces from one square to any arbitrarily selected square. Here one distinguishes the qualified chess player from the beginner. The beginner, in order to move a piece from one square to another, has to carry out some serious logical work, whereas the expert proceeds automatically.

When the beginning chess player who has just learned the rules of the game sits at the board, it is quite hard for him to construct a mathematical map of the position, since the task of moving the pieces requires logical work. To solve the problem of which movements of the pieces are possible, he has to construct and analyze the corresponding mathematical map, which allows him to come to a decision. So, the beginner has to divide his chess abilities between two tasks, that is between two mathematical maps: 1) the problem of which movements of the pieces are possible and 2) the proper chess problem of picking the best move.

The expert proceeds in a totally different fashion. The problem of which movements are possible he solves without thinking, that is, without putting together a mathematical representation. All of his chess abilities can be given over to the mathematical map of the position; this naturally leads to an extension of the horizon. How does the experienced player solve the problem of moving the pieces? As the reader has undoubtedly already conjectured, this question is far from being an idle one. It is directly connected with the education of the machine in the mastery of chess. If the machine solves the problem of moving the pieces by the same method as the master does, then the capabilities of the machine can be devoted to the selection of meaningful moves. If the machine has to devote a significant portion of its abilities to the rules of the game, then matters are worse and the horizon cannot be far off.

We may cite the following example, which should illuminate the heart of the matter. Let us imagine that a participant in a match for the championship of the world, having adjourned the game, sets out for a stroll. He continues blindly with his analysis of the position, constructing and analyzing the mathematical map; he does not distinguish the faces of the passersby that he meets and so does not recognize acquaintances, but he collides with no one. Moreover, he obeys all the traffic rules as he crosses the street, all the while keeping up his study. What is the meaning of this?

The fact is that the problem of moving his own body is solved by the grandmaster without loading his logical apparatus. He switches it over, as it were, to an automaton. In the same way, the experienced player automatically solves the problem of the possible movements of the pieces.

It may be that this auxiliary problem is solved by the principle of a handbook in which for every question (out of some collection of questions) there is an answer. If a problem must be solved over and over again, if it is a standard problem, it makes sense to solve it not by logic but by the handbook method. One must assume that this is the way man learns; this is apparently the way the machine should be taught the rules of the game.

Clichés—The Coding Tables

To construct a mathematical map with a given horizon we must know how to move a piece from a given square on the board to an arbitrary destination that it can reach in the given number of half-moves or less. We have to define the squares on the path of motion and the number of half-moves required for the piece to occupy these squares.

If an apparatus designed to play chess cannot do this, then it cannot compute the necessary mathematical functions and construct and analyze the mathematical map of the corresponding horizon.

Thus the "technical" algorithm, the algorithm for the rules of the game, must correspond to the logical algorithm and be adequate for it. What is the nature of man's ability to move pieces on the board and compute the number of half-moves?

We must suppose that this problem is solved by applying "cliches" (or coding tables) defining the moves of the pieces. Let us look first at the coding table for the movement of pieces on a board where there are no obstacles. Then we shall consider the same problem but with the addition of the boundary effect and subsequently with the inclusion of obstacles on the board (the presence of other pieces).

The pieces can be divided into two groups: one moving about on the board with constant velocity (the King, the Knight, and the Pawn) and the other that can move with variable velocity (the Queen, the Rook and the Bishop). We shall begin with pieces belonging to the first group.

The King The coding table for the moves of the King on a free board is shown in Fig. 4. It consists of 15 x 15=225 squares filled in with numbers. We shall take it that the initial position of the moving piece corresponds to the

+7	7	7	7	7	7	7	7	7	7	7	7	7	7	7	7
	7	6	6	6	6	6	6	6	6	6	6	6	6	6	7
	7	6	5	5	5	5	5	5	5	5	5	5	5	6	7
	7	6	5	4	4	4	4	4	4	4	4	4	5	6	7
	7	6	5	4	3	3	3	3	3	3	3	4	5	6	7
	7	6	5	4	3	2	2	2	2	2	3	4	5	6	7
	7	6	5	4	3	2	1	1	1	2	3	4	5	6	7
0	7	6	5	4	3	2	1	0	1	2	3	4	5	6	7
	7	6	5	4	3	2	1	1	1	2	3	4	5	6	7
	7	6	5	4	3	2	2	2	2	2	3	4	5	6	7
	7	6	5	4	3	3	3	3	3	3	3	4	5	6	7
	7	6	5	4	4	4	4	4	4	4	4	4	5	6	7
	7	6	5	5	5	5	5	5	5	5	5	5	5	6	7
	7	6	6	6	6	6	6	6	6	6	6	6	6	6	7
-7	7	7	7	7	7	7	7	7	7	7	7	7	7	7	7

     -7   0   +7

Fig. 4. The coding table for the moves of the King.

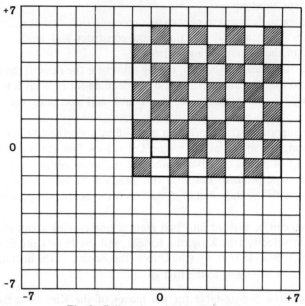

Fig. 5. Collocation of table and board.

square containing the number 0. The numbers in the other squares of the table indicate the number of moves necessary to move the King from the square numbered 0 to the given square.

We shall assume that the King is located on the square b2 and that it is necessary to determine the number of moves and the path of the King in going to the square at f7. To this end we locate the square b2 of the board at the zero square of the coding table in Fig. 4, in the way shown in Fig. 5. In this case the square f7 coincides with a square in the coding table containing the number 5. This "5" is the number of moves needed by the King. In order to define the movement path we must put the square f7 of the board on the zero square of the coding table in Fig. 4. In this case we find the square b2 on a square with the number 5 (this is natural, since the inverse path consists of five moves).

We have made two collocations. Each has defined on every square of the board a corresponding number; as a result every square on the board bears two numbers. The path of the King from b2 to f7 can include those squares whose numbers, corresponding to a particular collocation, change by unity and for which the sum of the two numbers (from the two collocations) is equal to 5. There may be several such paths. If, in moving, a piece comes to rest on a square in which the sum of the two numbers is not five but, say, six, this means that the path going through this square would require not five, but, as a minimum, six moves.

Thus we can find both the path of motion and the number of moves (displacements) of which the path consists when there are no obstacles, that is, when the board is free and unbounded. What can be done when the board is filled with pieces and the move also runs into the boundaries of the board?

For the solution of this practical task we may make use of the key shown in Fig. 6 (for the meaning of the symbols see Fig. 7). The dashed line refers to the impermissibility of occupying a square lying beyond the line; the black line on a square indicates that the square lies outside the board; the black triangle indicates that the square is occupied by a piece of the same color as the King, which is situated on the square 0.

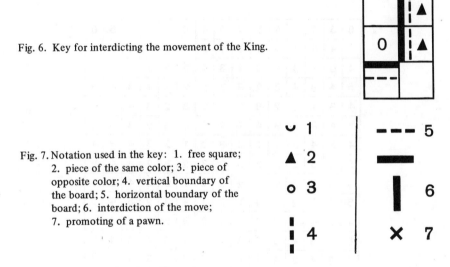

Fig. 6. Key for interdicting the movement of the King.

Fig. 7. Notation used in the key: 1. free square; 2. piece of the same color; 3. piece of opposite color; 4. vertical boundary of the board; 5. horizontal boundary of the board; 6. interdiction of the move; 7. promoting of a pawn.

This key prevents us from moving the King so that he occupies a square already occupied by pieces of his own side or so that he moves outside the board.

Let us now return to the example in which we move the King from the square b2 to the square f7. How will the King move if the board contains pieces of his own? Enemy pieces introduce no problem and they do not appear in the King's key.

When moving the King on a real board we need a reconnaissance just as we did on the free board. We locate the squares b2 and f7, one after the other at the zero square of the coding table, and we find those squares of the board on which the sum of the numbers is equal to five, and the number from square to square changes by unity. All the squares of the trajectory must have the sum five. If the trajectory cannot be made up from squares in which the numbers sum to five, either because the board is carrying pieces of the King's own color or because of the influence of the edge, then we must look for other squares. If it turns out that in a path there is one square with a sum equal to six or more, the path will consist of six or more moves. The numbers from square to square, as before, must change by unity.

The Knight   The coding table for the moves of the Knight is shown in Fig. 8 and the inhibition key in Fig. 9. Nothing essentially new appears in comparison with the movements of the King. We merely note that, although on the free board the boundary effect may limit the number of possible squares in the path of the King, it does not affect the number of moves; whereas for the Knight's move on a free board, the edge of the board does indeed affect the number of moves. For example, in Fig. 10 we show the code for the moves of a Knight on a

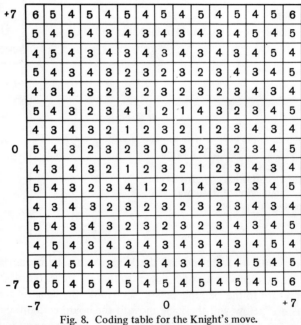

Fig. 8. Coding table for the Knight's move.

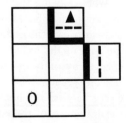

Fig. 9. Interdiction key for the Knight's move.

free board when he occupies the square b2. The coding table (Fig. 8) says that the square a1 may be reached by the Knight from the square b2 in two moves but only by going through a square on the coding table which lies outside the board. If we put the square a1 over the zero square on the coding table, it is clear that only two squares of the coding table which carry the number 1 also coincide with squares on the board. These are the squares at b3 and c2. Putting the square b2 at the zero square on the coding table shows that these squares correspond to the number 3. The sum of these numbers is equal to 4 and therefore the square a1 in Fig. 10 receives the number 4.

3	4	3	4	3	4	5	6
4	3	4	3	4	3	4	5
3	2	3	2	3	4	3	4
2	3	2	3	2	3	4	3
1	2	1	4	3	2	3	4
2	3	2	1	2	3	4	3
3	0	3	2	3	2	3	4
4	3	2	1	2	3	4	3

Fig. 10. The code for the moves of the Knight on the board.

The Pawn The coding tables for the Pawn moves are represented in Figs. 11 and 12, there being four tables in all! This is explained by the fact that the Black

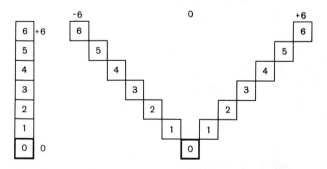

Fig. 11. Coding table for the moves of the White Pawn.

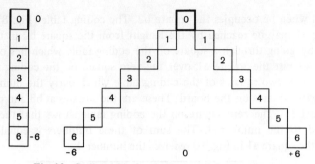

Fig. 12. Coding table for the moves of the Black Pawn.

and White Pawns move in different directions, and, moreover, that the move of
the Pawn changes when it makes a capture. The different coding tables require

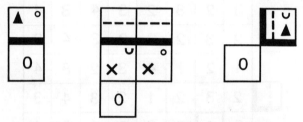

Fig. 13. Interdiction keys and the key for promotion
of the White Pawn.

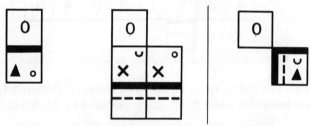

Fig. 14. Interdiction keys and the key for promotion
of the Black Pawn.

different inhibition keys (Figs. 13 and 14). The Pawn is the only piece having
keys for promotion. We note that the possibility of the double move of the
Pawn from the initial position and capture en passant have not been taken into
account in the construction of the coding table and the key for the Pawns. For
these two cases additional coding tables are needed, but for simplicity we will
not discuss them here. Since every Pawn has two coding tables, when we are
making up the code of Pawn moves on the board we need to use two tables and
three keys at each move. The concept of a free board loses most of its meaning
since a capture is possible only when the board is not free. The method of

searching for moves which was used in the cases of the King and the Knight has to be abandoned. But this method for simplifying the problem is not needed here; the Pawn movement is sufficiently primitive anyway. We must use the real board and successively place the zero square of the several coding tables on the square where the Pawn is standing and apply the corresponding keys and so construct the code for the Pawn moves on the real board.

The Queen   Here we come to a problem quite different in principle, since the Queen belongs to the class of pieces that can fight from afar, that can in one move traverse the entire board. Here we come to squares of type β. Such pieces can move with different velocities. The range of these pieces causes the coding table for the free board (see Fig. 15) to have no squares with a number greater than two. When we consider the real board, the method used for the King and the Knight is not applicable in its pure form, since it is difficult to define a number of moves necessary for the passage of the Queen (for example, five) if the coding table has no squares with a number greater than two.

+7														
1	2	2	2	2	2	2	1	2	2	2	2	2	2	1
2	1	2	2	2	2	2	1	2	2	2	2	2	1	2
2	2	1	2	2	2	2	1	2	2	2	2	1	2	2
2	2	2	1	2	2	2	1	2	2	2	1	2	2	2
2	2	2	2	1	2	2	1	2	2	1	2	2	2	2
2	2	2	2	2	1	2	1	2	1	2	2	2	2	2
2	2	2	2	2	2	1	1	1	2	2	2	2	2	2
1	1	1	1	1	1	1	0	1	1	1	1	1	1	1
2	2	2	2	2	2	1	1	1	2	2	2	2	2	2
2	2	2	2	2	1	2	1	2	1	2	2	2	2	2
2	2	2	2	1	2	2	1	2	2	1	2	2	2	2
2	2	2	1	2	2	2	1	2	2	2	1	2	2	2
2	2	1	2	2	2	2	1	2	2	2	2	1	2	2
2	1	2	2	2	2	2	1	2	2	2	2	2	1	2
1	2	2	2	2	2	2	1	2	2	2	2	2	2	1

−7   −7   0   +7

Fig. 15. The coding table for the Queen's moves.

In order to simplify the task of moving the Queen and other long-range pieces on a real board, we shall limit ourselves to the search for paths of three moves. Among other things, this is not such a small accomplishment as it would appear at first sight. An experiment which will be carried out later shows that in complex positions grandmasters limit themselves to moving the pieces for as little as two moves.

The three-move paths may be searched out by the following method: 1) we put the square b2 of the board on the zero square of the coding table and we mark out the squares with the number 1 (to do this we have to make use of the key given in Fig. 16, and the squares of the board lying behind the dashed lines will be left unnumbered); 2) we put the square f7 of the board on the zero

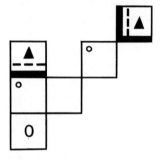

Fig. 16. Interdiction key for the Queen.

square of the coding table and perform the same operation (in these cases we obtain two sets of squares bearing the number 1); 3) we successively put the squares of the first set on the zero square, and we develop a third set of squares bearing the number 1; 4) if the squares of the first set coincide with squares of the second set, then the coinciding squares are included in a path made up of three Queen moves. This method is universal; it can be extended to the movement of the King and the Knight, and if we look ahead a bit, we can say that it can be extended to the movement of the Rook and the Bishop.

For two-move paths, the matter is somewhat simpler. We have shown in Fig. 17 the code for the moves of the Queen from the square b2 on a real board where the square e2 and f6 are occupied by pieces of the same color. Then on the squares f6, g7, h8, e2, f2, g2, and h2, where there are 1's on the free board, the circumstances are changed. The squares f6 and e2 are under interdiction and the number 2 appears on the squares g7, h8, f2, g2 and h2, as can easily be seen by the use of coincidental sets of squares.

2	1	2	2	2	2	2	2
2	1	2	2	2	2	2	2
2	1	2	2	2	▲	2	2
2	1	2	2	1	2	2	2
2	1	2	1	2	2	2	2
1	1	1	1	2	2	2	2
1	0	1	1	▲	2	2	2
1	1	1	2	2	2	2	2

Fig. 17. Code for the moves of the Queen on the board.

The Rook   In this case, we have to use the coding table of Fig. 18 and the key of Fig. 19. The method of defining paths of three moves is the same as for the Queen.

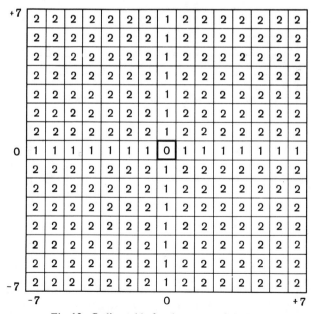

Fig. 18. Coding table for the moves of the Rook.

Fig. 19. Interdiction key for the Rook.

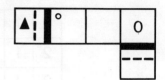

The Bishop   In this case, we use the table of Fig. 20 and the key of Fig. 21. The method is the same as for the Queen and the Rook.

	-7	-6	-5	-4	-3	-2	-1	0	1	2	3	4	5	6	7
+7	1		2		2		2		2		2		2		1
		1		2		2		2		2		2		1	
	2		1		2		2		2		2		1		2
		2		1		2		2		2		1		2	
	2		2		1		2		2		1		2		2
		2		2		1		2		1		2		2	
	2		2		2		1		1		2		2		2
0		2		2		2		0		2		2		2	
	2		2		2		1		1		2		2		2
		2		2		1		2		1		2		2	
	2		2		1		2		2		1		2		2
		2		1		2		2		2		1		2	
	2		1		2		2		2		2		1		2
		1		2		2		2		2		2		1	
-7	1		2		2		2		2		2		2		1

       -7   0   + 7

Fig. 20. Coding table for the moves of the Bishop.

Fig. 21. Interdiction key for the Bishop.

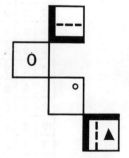

And so, dear reader, we have together learned how to move the pieces from one arbitrary square to another (with the exception of castling and the two-square Pawn move which we noted earlier), provided that no more than three moves are needed. This is an outstanding achievement, since the electronic computer, according to the mathematicians, knows how to move the pieces for one move only. Since we now know how to solve the problem of making the possible moves, and since the problem of selecting variations that make sense was solved in the previous chapter, we can now go on to a test of our algorithm.

An Experiment

As an example of play for annihilation, let us look at a position from the well-known game of Botvinnik-Capablanca (Rotterdam, 1938). At the time, the combination which emerged in this game aroused delight in the chess world. This combination can be easily found by the methods developed in this book.

In the position shown in Fig. 22, White is to move. Let us construct the *map for one half-move.*

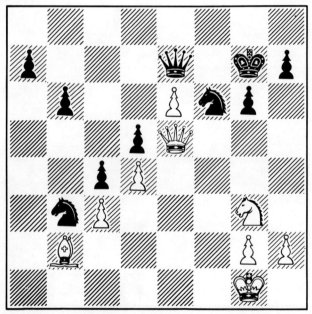

Fig. 22. Position: Botvinnik-Capablanca, Rotterdam, 1938.

First we must solve the technical problem of determining all the attacks that White can make in one half-move. In other words, we must define all the displacements of the White pieces that can be made in one move. In order not to bore the reader with this tedious work, we shall determine only the most difficult—the displacements of the White Queen. Putting the square e5 of the board on the zero square of the coding table given in Fig. 15 and using the key of Fig. 16, we obtain the code for the White Queen, as shown in Fig. 23. An inspection of this code indicates that there are only two squares on the board (d5 and f6) where the number 1 appears and where there are also enemy pieces. Therefore, in the mathematical map for one half-move, there occur only two Queen moves (out of the 27 that are theoretically possible on the free board).

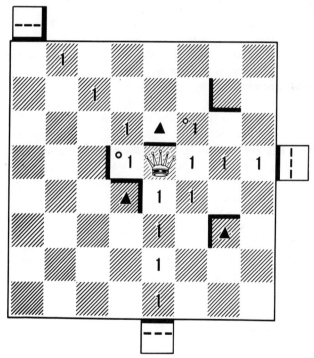

Fig. 23. Code for the Queen moves from square e5 in the initial position shown in Fig. 22.

It is not hard to see that there are no other captures in one half-move; thus we may construct the first mathematical map.

Values:

$Qe5-jKtf6\cdot0(1)\cdot1(e5)\cdot1(f6)-jPd5\cdot0(1)\cdot1(e5)\cdot1(d5)$.

The expression $0(1)$ refers to the function ψ. This function is equal to 0, and the "1" in parentheses refers to the fact that there remains one half-move before the value becomes $\psi=1$.

The expression 1(e5) refers to the value of the function f=1 at e5 in the attack paths. Since the play is for one half-move, all the functions of the α-squares in the attack paths are equal to 1, and there are no retreat paths.

The scan is carried out over only those moves which occur in the map, that is, the paths over which the pieces are displaced. There are only two such moves: (1) 1. Q:f6 and (2) 1. Q:b5. We shall look at these possibilities in turn.

(1) 1. Qe5:f6   Properly speaking, here we must again define all the captures possible in one half-move, which lets us take account of changes, and continue the analysis of the mathematical map. The reader has in all probability already noted the definition of the possible moves, the construction, and the analysis of the map; all this composes the process of "thinking" in the apparatus that is engaged here in playing chess. But, since the reader has already become convinced that the discovery of the possible displacements of pieces in one move is an elementary task, we shall omit this operation until we meet the need to make up the map for three half-moves; then we shall have to work out the displacements of the pieces in two moves.

There are now new values:

jKg7–Qf6·0 (1)·1 (g7)·1 (f6)

jQe7–Qf6·0(1)·1 (e7)·1 (f6)–Pe6.0 (1)·1 (e7)·1 (e6)

jKtb3–Pd4·0 (1)·1 (b3)·1 (d4)

Thus, there are three possible answers to the move 1. Q:f6.

1 . . . Ktb3:d4. We may avoid the computation of new values since Formula (9″) yields | jKtf6 | > | Pd4 | · 1·1, that is 3 > 1, and the variation 1. Q:f6 Kt:d4 is disadvantageous for Black.

1 . . . Qe7:f6. There are no new values for White. The formula (9′) indicates |jKtf6 | – |Qf6 |< 0, 3–9 < 0 and the variation is disadvantageous for White.

1 . . . Kg7:f6. The estimate is the same as for 1 . . . Q:f6.

In summary, the variations 1. Q:f6 Q:f6 and 1. Q:f6 K:f6 are advantageous to Black and the move 1. Q:f6 is rejected.

(2) 1. Qe5:d5   New values:

jQe7–Pe6·0(1)·1(e7)·1(e6)

jKtf6–Qd5·0(1)·1(f6)·1(d5)

jKtb3–Pd4·0(1)·1(b3)·1(d4)

Thus, Black again has three answers to the move 1. Q:d5 1 . . . Ktb3:d4. New values:

Qd5–jKtd4·0(1)·1(d5)·1(d4)–jPc4·0(1)·1(d5)·1(c4)

In the case 2, Qd5:d4 we obtain the value:

jQe7–Pe6.0(1).1(e7).1(e6)

Formula (9″) yields | jPd5+jKtd4 | – | Pd4 | > | Pe6 | .1.1, i.e., 3 > 1, and the variant 1. Q:d5 Kt:d4 is disadvantageous for Black.

1 . . . Qe7:e6. The new values are:

Qd5–jPc4 0(1)·1(d5)·1(c4)–jQe6·0(1)·1(d5)·1(e6)

It is sufficient to consider 2. Q:e6, after which we have one value:
jKtb3–Pd4.0(1).1(b3).1(d4)

Formula (9″) says | jPd5+jQe6 | − |Pe6 | > | Pd4 | .1.1, that is 9 > 1 and the variant is unfavorable for Black.

1... Ktf6:d5 There are no new values.

Formula (9″) yields | jPd5 | − | Qd5 | < 0, 1 − 9 < 0, and the variant 1. Q:d5 Kt:d5 is unfavorable to White; the move 1. Q:d5 is refuted.

Thus, on the basis of the map for one half-move, all the variations are in favor of Black! We therefore develop the *map for two half-moves*.
The values:

$$\text{Qe5} - j\text{Ktf6} \cdot 0\ (1) \cdot 1\ (\text{e5})\ [1\ (\text{f6}) + (0 - 1) \cdot 1\ \frac{1\ (j\text{Kg7})}{(j\text{Qe7})} \cdot 1\ (\text{f6})] \cdot 1$$

$$- j\text{Pd5} \cdot 0\ (1) \cdot 1\ (\text{e5}) \cdot [1\ (\text{d5}) + (0 - 1) \cdot 1\ (j\text{Ktf6}) \cdot 1\ (\text{d5})]$$

jQe7 − Pe6·0 (2) ·1 (e7) ·1 (e6) · [1 − 0 (e7)]
jKtb3 − Pd4·0 (2) ·1 (b3) ·1 (d4) · [1 − 0 (d5)]

Formula (7) was used in the construction of the expressions in brackets, which we used in computing the intangible value of the Queen at e5. The pieces in parentheses, (jQe7) and (jKg7), are negating pieces. The expressions [1 − 0 (e7)] and [1 − 0 (d5)] make up the retreat path − see Formula (7). The expression 1 (jQe7) refers to a double negation, which may be denoted by 0^2.

　　　1 (jKg7)

As before, White has two moves:

(1) 1. Qe5:d5　The new values are:
Qd5–jPc4·0(2)· [1(d5)+(0−1)·1(jKtf6)·1(d5)] ·1(c4)· [1−0(c3)]
jQe7–Pe6·0(1)·1(e7)· {1(e6)+(0−1)· [1(Qd5)+(0−1)·1(jKtf6)·1(d5)}
jKtf6–Qd5·0(1)·1(f6) 1(d5)
jKtb3–Pd4·0(1)·1(b3)·[1(d4)+(0−1)·1(Pc3)·1(d4)]

After the possible move 1... Kt:d5, as determined by the map, Formula (9′) yields | jPd5 | < | Qd5 | ·1·1, i.e., 1 < 9 and the move 1. Q:d5 should be abandoned.

(2) 1. Qe5:f6　This is another possibility, and there are different values:
Qf6–jKg7·0(2)·[1(f6)+(0−1)·1(jQe7)·1(f6)] ·1(g7)
　　　　　　　1(jKg7)
−jQe7·0(2)·[1(f6)+(0−1)·1(jQe7)·1(f6)] ·1(e7)
　　　　　　　1(jKg7)
jQe7–Qf6·0(1)·1(e7)·1(f6)–Pe6·0(1)·1(e7)·
　· {1(e6)+(0−1)·[1(Qf6)+(0−1)·1(jQe7)·1(f6)] ·1(e6)1}
　　　　　　　1(jKg7)
jKg7–Qf6·0(1)·1(g7)·1(f6)

For the responses that must be considered, namely 1... Q:f6 and 1... K:f6 Formula (9′) yields | jKtf6 | < | Qf6 | ·1·1, or 3 < 9, and the variation is not good for White. Nor does carrying the play to two half-moves bring in anything new.

It is necessary to go further and construct the map for three half-moves, where the pieces will be displaced by two moves. This is a more difficult task than to displace them by one move. It is of interest, therefore, to see how we go about the discovery of the possible moves. Let us begin with the White Queen.

To determine the possible captures by the White Queen in two moves, we must construct the code of moves of the Queen on the board for one move from e5, and then the codes of Queen moves from all the squares containing enemy pieces. If squares belonging to the set of squares bearing the number 1 in the code originating with the Queen at e5 coincide with squares belonging to another set bearing the number 1 in a code originating with the Queen at a square occupied by an enemy piece, that piece can be captured in two moves and the attack falls inside the mathematical map.

The code for Queen moves originating at e5 is already known (Fig. 23). We must now construct the codes for Queen moves from the squares containing enemy pieces.

Let us construct them from origins at g7 and e7; in other words, let us see whether the Queen at e5 can attack the King at g7 and the Queen at e7 in two moves.

The code for g7 is displayed in Fig. 24. Comparing the so-developed set of squares bearing the number 1 with the set from Fig. 23, we see that there is only

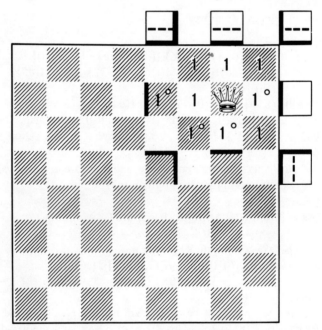

Fig. 24. Code for the moves of the Queen from square g7.

one common square bearing the number 1, the square at f6. The Queen's attack path against the Black King, from e5 to g7, has been found to be (e5-f6-g7) and this is the only path.

Comparing the sets of squares bearing the number 1 in Figs. 23 and 25, we find three attack paths for the White Queen at e5 against the Black Queen at e7, via any one of the squares c7, d6, and f6.

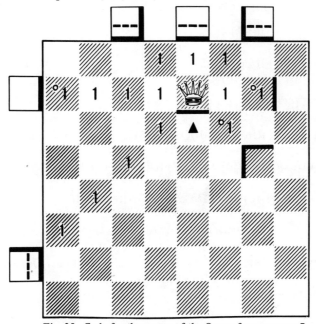

Fig. 25. Code for the moves of the Queen from square e7.

We need not include other attacks, since the problem is not complex; we may now construct and analyze the map. It is worthwhile, however, to remember that the subsidiary task that we have just abandoned is absolutely necessary, and that it forms a single whole with the construction and analysis of the map (see p. 00, where the map for three half-moves is given).

How the value of White's pieces has grown, in both quantity and quality! Black, on the other hand, has merely refined his values.

At the outset, White had 27 possible moves. The mathematical map for three half-moves shows that only twelve of them are meaningful. We must now determine whether these twelve satisfy Formula (9′), that is, whether they lead to meaningful variations.

(1) 1. Qe5:f6 We shall not construct a new map, even though one would be required if we were to be strictly accurate. We shall use the old map, where the move 1. Q:f6 is twice refuted, and we shall consider one of the negations, namely 1. . . Qe7:f6. There are new values for White:

Pe6—(Qe8–Pe8)·0(3)· [1(e7)+(0–1)·1(*j*Qf6)·1(e7)]

$\cdot\begin{bmatrix} 1(e8)+(0-1)\cdot1(jKg7)\cdot1(f8)\cdot1(e8) \\ \cdot1(Qf6)\cdot1(f8)\cdot1(e8) \end{bmatrix}$

Ktg3–*j*Qf6.0(3). $\begin{bmatrix} 1(h5)+(0-1)\cdot1(jPg6)\cdot1(h5) \\ 1(e4)+(0-1)\cdot1(jPd5)\cdot1(e4) \end{bmatrix}$

·1(f6)· [1–1(........)]

–*j*Kg7·0(3)·$\begin{bmatrix} 1(h5)+(0-1)\cdot1(jPg6)\cdot1(h5) \\ 1(f5)+(0-1)\cdot1(jPg6)\cdot1(f5) \end{bmatrix}$

·1(g7)·[1–1(......)]

Qe5–*j*Ktf6·0(1)·1(e5)·[1(f6)+(0–1)·1(*j*Qe7)·1(f6)]
1(*j*Kg7)
–*j*Kg7·0(3)·1(e5)·[1(f6)+(0–1)·1(*j*Qe7)·1(f6] ·1(g7)·[1–1(f8, g8, h8, h6)]
1(*j*Kg7)
–*j*Qe7·0(3)·1(e5)·[1(f6)+(0–1)·1(*j*Qe7)·1(f6)] ·1(e7)·[1–1(...........)]
1(*j*Kg7)
[1(d6)+(0–1)·1(*j*Qe7)·1(d6)] ·1(e7)·[1–1(...........)]
[1(c7)+(0–1)·1(*j*Qe7)·1(c7)] ·1(e7)·[1–1(...........)]
–*j*Pa7·0(3)·1(e5)·1(b8)   ·[1(a7)+(0–1)·1(*j*Qe7)·1(a7)]·[1–1(a6, a5)]
[1(c7)+(0–1)·1(*j*Qe7)·1(c7)]
–*j*Pb6·0(3)·1(e5)·1(b8)   ·[1(b6)+(0–1)·1(*j*Pa7)·1(b6)]·[1–1(b5)]
[1(c7)+(0–1)·1(*j*Qe7)·1(c7)]
[1(d6+(0–1)·1(*j*Qe7)·1(d6)]
–*j*Pc4·0(3)·1(e5)·[1(d5)+(0–1)·1(*j*Ktf6)·1(d5)] ·1(c4)·[1–0(c3)]
[1(c7)+(0–1)·1(*j*Qe7)·1(c7)] ·[1(c4)+(0–1)·1(*j*Pd5)·1(c4)] ·[1–0(c3)]
–*j*Pd5·0(1)·1(e5)·[1(d5)+(0–1)·1(*j*Ktf6)·1(d5)]
–*j*Pg6·0(3)·1(e5)·1(g5)   ·[1(g6)+(0–1)·1(*j*Kg7)·1(g6)]·[1–0(g5)]
[1(f5)+(0–1)·1(*j*Pg6)·1(f5)]   1(*j*Ph7)
[1(h5)+(1–0)·1(*j*Pg6)·1(h5)]
–*j*Ph7·0(3)·1(e5)·[1(h5)+(0–1)·1(*j*Pg6)·1(h5)] ·[1(h7)+(0–1)·1(*j*Kg7)·1(h7)]·[1–1(h6)]
Ktg3–*j*Kg7·0(3)·1(g3)·[1(f5)+(0–1)·1(*j*Pg6)·1(f5)]·1(g7)·[1–1(f8, g8, h8)]
[1(h5)+(0–1)·1(*j*Pg6)·1(h5)]
–*j*Ktf6·0(3)·1(g3)·[1(h5)+(0–1)·1(*j*Pg6)·1(h5)] ·1(f6)·[1–1(.........)]
[1(e4)+(0–1)·1(*j*Pd5)·1(e4)]
–*j*Qe7·0(3)·1(g3)·[1(f5)+(0–1)·1(*j*Pg6)·1(f5)] ·1(e7)·[1–1(...........)]
Ba3–*j*Qe7·0(3)·1(b2)·[1(a3)+(0–1)·1(Qe7)·1(a3)] ·1(e7)·[1–1(.........)]
*j*Ktb3–Pd4·0(2)·1(b3)·[1(d4)+(0–1)·1(Qe5)·1(d4)] ·[1–0(d5)]
1(Pc3)·1(d4)
*j*Qe7–Pe6·0(2)1(e7)–[1(e6)+(0–1)·1(Qe5)·1(e6)]·[1–0(e7)]

In order to satisfy the condition stipulated in Formula (9′), White has only two possible moves – 2. Kth5 and 2. Ktf5. After the replies 2. . . gh and 2. . . gf, which are meaningful moves according to the map, the variation 1. Q:f6 turns out to be disadvantageous for White.

(2)–(8) In a similar way, the variations beginning with the moves 1. Qb8, 1. Qc7, 1. Qd6, 1. Q:d5, 1. Qf5, 1. Qg5, and 1. Qh5 are refuted. Black moves according to the map, and Formula (9′) produces a negative result.

(9) 1: Ktg3 – e4 According to the map, Black replies with 1. . . de. As in the cases (1) - (8), Formula (9′) testifies against the move 1. Kte4.

(10) 1. Ktg3 – f5 The map recommends 1. . . gf.
Here White has a new value:
Qe5 – jKg7·0(3)·1 (e5)·1 (g3)·1 (g7)·(1-1)
So, 1. Qg3.
In accordance with the map, Black may reply by 2. . . Kh8. White may now continue with 3. Qg8, 3. Qg7, 3. Qd6, 3. Qc7. All of these will be terminated by Formula (9′) as unsatisfactory after the obvious answers by Black, according to the map. After 3. Ba3, Black may answer with 3. . . Q:e6 and the only variation 4. Qb8 Kte8 (Ktg8) is rejected by Formula (9′). There remains only 3. Qb8, but then in accordance with the map. (Probably the reader has already conjectured that we are not writing out all those new values that necessarily appear.) 3. . . Kte8 4. Qe5 Qf6, and White can no longer obtain a favorable orientation of the inequality in Formula (9′).

(11) 1. Ktg3 – h5 According to the map, the answer should be 1. . . gh. For the time being, Formula (9′) says that the scan of the move should be continued since γ = +1 (through the intangible value of the attack by the Queen at e5 on the King at g7) since the Pawn at g6 is displaced to a new square and a new value appears:
Qe5 – jKg7·0 (3)·1 (e5)·1 (g5)·1 (g7)· [1-1 (f8, h8)]
Thus, 2. Qg5 and Black has only the answer 2. . . Kh8 (2. . . Kf8 will not be considered since after 3. Ba3 Q:a3 the situation is reduced to the scan of 12 which will be given later.)

Now, White cannot get a favorable value for Formula (9′) because, for instance, of 3. Ba3 Q:e6, and so on.

There still remains for consideration a move corresponding to the map and carrying a favorable value for Formula (9′), namely, 2. Ba3 (after 1. Kth5 gh). Then 2. . . Qe8 (2. . . Q:a3 will be examined later) and it is not difficult to see that the scan must be broken off in favor of Black.

Thus, there remains the final move in the initial position.

(12) 1. Bb2· – a3 Black has several alternatives (see the position in Fig. 26):

the moves 1...Q:e6, 1...Qc7, 1...Ktc5, 1...Kt:d4, 1...Ktg4 and 1...Ktd7 are immediately ruled out. A new map appears and Formula (9″) is applied. We now have the moves 1...Qb7, 1...Qd8, 1...Qe8, and 1...Q:a3 to be examined.

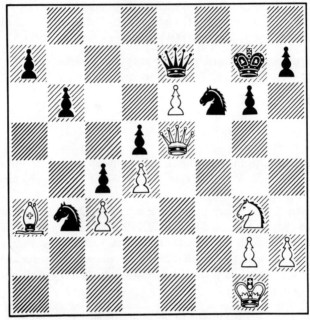

Fig. 26. Position after move 1. Ba3.

1...Qb7 White has several possibilities. By constructing the map and applying Formula (9′) we can choose two advantageous continuations, for example, 2. Bf8 and 2. Kth5. These moves must be examined since they are included in the map.

To save space we shall consider only 2. Kth5. This move satisfies the condition (9′) since after the capture of the Knight at h5, there appears a new intangible value for the Queen at e5, namely:

$$-jKg7 \cdot 0(3) \cdot 1 \cdot 1 \cdot 1(1-1)$$

and $-|\text{Kth5}| > -(1-\Theta) \cdot |jKg7| \cdot \gamma$

So, 2...gh 3. Qg5 Kh8 4. Q:f6 Qg7 5. Qd8 Qg8 6. e7. For Black, all moves are forced answers. 1...Qb7 leads to a gain for White.

We have a similar evaluation for 1...Qd8 and 1...Qe8. It can be said in general that the three moves 1...Qb7, 1...Qe8 and 1...Qd8 lead to an increase in the intangible values in the three-half-move map for the two pieces Ba3 and Pe6; for 1...Qe8 and 1...Qb7 there is a further increase in the intangible value of the Queen at e5.

We therefore consider
1... Q:a3 (see the position in Fig. 27).

Fig. 27. Position after move 1 . . . Q: a3.

The possibilities are 2. Qc7, 2. Qd6, 2. Q:f6, 2. Ktf5, and 2. Kth5. We shall look at 2. Kth5 (see Fig. 28).

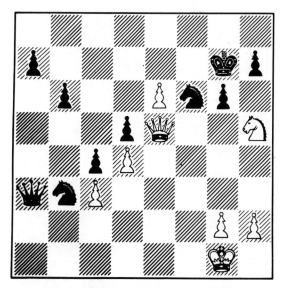

Fig. 28. Position after the move 2. Kth5.

Black has one answer: 2. . . gh (see Fig. 29).

White continues to play in accordance with the three-half-move map and Black has only the forced answers: 3. Qg5 Kf8 (or Kh8) 4. Q:f6 Kg8 (see Fig. 30).

Fig. 29. Position after the move 2 . . . gh.

Fig. 30. Position after the move 4 . . . Kg8.

There is a branching scan: 4. Ke8 5. Qf7 Kd8 6. Qd7; this is easily found by the standard methods, and rejected. We continue with 5. e7 (see Fig. 31).

Formula (9′) yields:

$- |P + K| > - |Qe8 - Pe8|.1.1$

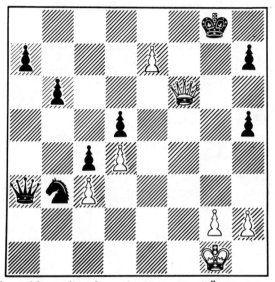

And, to get a favorable reading from the inequality (9″) Black has to attack the White King. Therefore Black must move 5... Qc1 6. Kf2 Qc2 (Qd2) 7. Kg3 Qd3 (Qe3) 8. Kh4 Qe4 (Qe1) 9. K:h5 Qe2 (see Fig. 32) are forced.

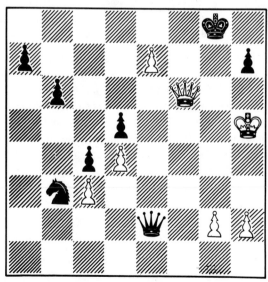

At no time could Black play Qg6, attacking the White Queen, since after the exchange of Queens Black loses his last chance—to smother the White King, i.e. to move the term $(1-F) \cdot |\mathrm{K}| \cdot \gamma = 200$ to the right hand side of the inequality (9″).

There is a branch. We may look at 10. Kh4 Qe4 11. g4 Qe1 12. Kh5 (see Fig. 33).

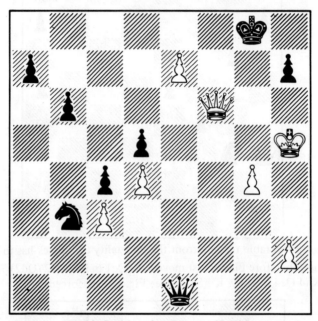

Fig. 33. Position after the move 12. Kh5.

Black can no longer maintain the leftward inequality sign (<) in (9″); the inequality is forced to change to (>) and the game is over, since as soon as White gets the move, the Black King is dead in three half-moves.

The reader will have noticed that we have not written down all the intangible values, nor all the formulae. The omissions were made to save space. The mathematical maps left out the β-squares in the paths that we studied. This was done to simplify the whole situation and to save space. In the event, the simplifications did not affect the results.

Examples for Analysis

Here are 60 positions for study. They are taken mainly from my own practice.

Openings

No.	Move		
1.	W	W.	Ke1, Qf3, Ra1, h1, Bc1, c4, Ktc3, g1, Pa2, b2, c2, d2, d5, g2, h2 (15).
		B.	Ke8, Qd8, Ra8, h8, Bc8, d6, Ktb8, f6, Pa7, b7, c6, f7, f4, g7, h7 (15).
2.	W	W.	Ke1, Qe2, Ra1, h1, Bc1, c4, Ktb1, f3, Pa2, b2, c2, d2, g2, h2 (14).
		B.	Kf8, Qd8, Ra8, h8, Bc8, d6, Ktb8, f6, Pa7, c6, f4, f7, g7, h7 (14).
3.	W	W.	Ke1, Qd1, Ra1, h1, Bc1, c4, Ktb1, f3, Pa2, c3, d4, e4, f2, g2, h2 (15).
		B.	Ke8, Qd8, Ra8, h8, Ba5, c8, Ktc6, g8, Pa7, b7, c7, d6, e5, f7, g7, h7 (16).
4.	W	W.	Kg1, Qd1, Ra1, e1, Bb3, c1, Ktb1, f3 Pa2, b2, c3, d2, e4, f2, g2, h3 (16).
		B.	Kg8, Qd8, Ra8, f8, Bc8, e7, Ktc6, f6, Pa6, b5, c7, d6, e5, f7, g7, h6 (16).

53

5.	W	W.	Kg1, Qd1, Ra1, e5, Bb3, c1, Ktb1, Pa2, b2, c3, d2, f2, g2, h2 (14).
		B.	Kg8, Qd8, Ra8, f8, Bc8, e7, Ktd5, Pa6, b5, c6, f7, g7, h7 (13).
6.	W	W.	Kg1, Qd1, Ra1, f1, Bb3, c1, Kte2, g3, Pa2, b2, c2, d4, f4, g2, h2 (15).
		B.	Ke8, Qd7, Ra8, h8, Bf8, g6, Ktb6, f6, Pa7, b7, c6, e6, f7, g7, h7 (15).
7.	W	W.	Ke1, Qd1, Ra1, h1, Be3, f1, Ktc3, Pa2, b2, c4, e4, f2, g2, h2 (14).
		B.	Ke8, Qd8, Ra8, h8, Bc8, g7, Ktd4, Pa7, b7, d7, e5, f7, g6, h7 (14).
8.	B	W.	Ke1, Qd1, Ra1, h1, Bc1, f1, Ktc3, f3, Pa2, b2, c2, d4, e5, f4, g2, h4 (16).
		B.	Kg8, Qd8, Ra8, f8, Bc8, g7, Ktb8, d7, Pa7, b7, c7, d6, e7, f7, g6, h7 (16).
9.	W	W.	Kd1, Qh5, Ra1, h1, Bc1, f1, Ktg1, Pa3, c2, c3, e5, f2, g2, h2 (14).
		B.	Kd8, Qc7, Ra8, g8, Bd7, Ktb8, e7, Pa7, b7, d4, d5, e6, f5 (13).
10.	B	W.	Ke1, Qd1, Ra1, h1, Bf1, f4, Ktc3, g1, Pa2, b2, d4, e3, f2, g4, h2 (15).
		B.	Ke8, Qd8, Ra8, h8, Be7, f5, Ktb8, g8, Pa7, b7, c6, d5, f7, g7, h7 (15).
11.	B	W.	Ke1, Qd1, Ra1, h1, Bb5, f4, Ktc3, f3, Pa2, b2, d4, e3, f2, g2, h2 (15).
		B.	Ke8, Qd8, Ra8, h8, Bf5, f8, Ktc6, f6, Pa7, b7, d5, e6, f7, g7, h7 (15).
12.	B	W.	Ke1, Qd1, Ra1, h1, Bc1, d3, Ktc3, f3, Pa2, b2, d5, e4, f2, g2, h2 (15).
		B.	Ke8, Qd8, Ra8, h8, Bc8, f8, Ktd7, f6, Pa6, b5, c5, e6, f7, g7, h7 (15).

13.   B   W.   Ke1, Qd1, Ra1, h1, Bc1, g2, Ktc3, g1, Pa2, b2, c4, d3, e4, f2, g3, h2 (16).

                    B.   Kg8, Qd8, Ra8, e8, Bc8, b4, Ktb8, f6, Pa7, b7, c7, d7, e5, f7, g7, h7 (16).

14.   B   W.   Ke1, Qa4, Ra1, h1, Bf1, Ktc3, g5, Pa2, b2, d4, d5, e2, f2, g2, h2 (15).

                    B.   Ke8, Qd8, Ra8, h8, Bc8, g7, Ktb8, Pa7, b7, c7, e6, f7, g6, h7 (14).

15.   B   W.   Ke1, Qh6, Ra1, h1, Bc1, f1, Ktg1, Pa3, c3, c4, d4, e3, f2, g2, h2 (15).

                    B.   Ke8, Qd8, Ra8, h8, Bc8, Ktb8, e4, Pa7, b7, c7, d7, e6, f5, g6, h7 (15).

16.   B   W.   Ke1, Qd1, Ra1, h1, Bb2, c4, Ktg1, Pa3, c3, d4, e3, f2, g2, h2 (14).

                    B.   Ke8, Qd8, Ra8, f8, Bc8, Ktb8, f6, Pa7, b7, c5, e6, f7, g7, h7 (14).

17.   B   W.   Kg1, Qd1, Ra1, f1, Be3, g2, Ktc3, f3, Pa2, b2, c4, d4, e4, f2, g3, h2 (16).

                    B.   Kg8, Qd8, Ra8, f8, Bc8, g7, Ktd7, f6, Pa7, b7, c6, d6, e5, f7, g6, h7 (16).

18.   W   W.   Ke1, Qd1, Ra1, h1, Be3, f1, Ktc3, g1, Pa2, b2, c4, d4, e4, f3, g2, h2 (16).

                    B.   Kg8, Qd8, Ra8, f8, Bc8, g7, Ktb8, f6, Pa7, b6, c7, d6, e7, f7, g6, h7 (16).

19.   B   W.   Kg1, Qd1, Ra1, f1, Bc1, g2, Ktd2, f3, Pa2, b2, c4, d4, e2, f2, g3, h2 (16).

                    B.   Kg8, Qd8, Ra8, f8, Bc8, e7, Ktb8, f6, Pa7, b7, c7, d5, e6, f5, g7, h7 (16).

20.   W   W.   Kg1, Qd1, Ra1, f1, Bc1, g2, Ktc3, f3, Pa2, b2, c4, d4, e2, f2, g3, h2 (16).

                    B.   Kg8, Qd8, Ra8, f8, Bb7, e7, Ktb8, e4, Pa7, b6, c7, d7, e6, f7, g7, h7 (16).

The Middle Game

21.   B   W.   Kf1, Qc2, Rd1, h1, Bf4, Ktc3, Pa2, b3, c4, d4, e2, f3, g3, h4 (14).

               B.   Kg8, Qg6, Ra8, f8, Bb4, d7, Pa7, b7, c6, d5, e4, e6, g7, h7 (14).

22.   B   W.   Ke3, Rc1, g4, Ba7, Ktc2, Pa2, d4, e5, g2, h2 (10).

               B.   Ke8, Rc8, h8, Bd7, Ktd2, Pc3, f7, g5, h6 (9).

23.   W   W.   Kg1, Qe2, Rc1, d1, Bb3, Ktc3, e5, Pa2, b2, d4, f3, g2, h2 (13).

               B.   Kg8, Qd8, Rc8, f8, Bb7, Kte7, f6, Pa7, b6, e6, f7, g7, h7 (13).

24.   W   W.   Kg1, Rd1, f2, Bg2, Pa4, b3, e5, f4, g3, h4 (10).

               B.   Kg8, Rd4, Bd3, e7, Pa7, b4, c2, e6, f5, g7, h7 (11).

25.   B   W.   Kg1, Qd2, Rc1, d1, Be3, Ktc3, Pa2, e2, c5, d5, f4, g2, h2 (13).

               B.   Kg8, Qa5, Ra8, d8, Bg7, Ktf6, Pa7, b7, f3, f7, g6, h7 (12).

26.   B   W.   Kg1, Qc2, Ra1, f1, Bf4, Ktc3, c4, Pa2, b2, d4, e3, f2, g3, h2 (14).

               B.   Kg8, Qb7, Ra8, d8, Be7, Ktc6, f6, Pa7, b6, c7, e6, f7, g7, h7 (14).

27.   W   W.   Kg1, Qe2, Ra1, f1, Bb2, d3, Ktd1, e5, Pa2, c4, d4, f4, g2, h2 (14).

               B.   Kg8, Qc7, Ra7, d8, Bb7, e7, Ktf6, f8, Pa6, b6, e6, f7, g7, h7 (14).

28.   W   W.   Kg2, Qf3, Rd1, d3, Ktc3, Pa4, b3, c4, d4, e5, g3, h2 (12).

               B.   Kg8, Qe7, Rd7, e8, Bg5, Pa7, b7, c6, e6, f5, g7, h7 (12).

29. W   W. Kg1, Qe4, Ra1, e1, Bf3, Pa2, c3, c4, d4, e3, f2, g2, h2 (13).

         B. Kg8, Qf6, Ra8, e8, Ktc6, Pa7, b7, c5, d6, e5, f7, g7, h6 (13).

30. W   W. Kg1, Qc2, Rc1, Ktf3, Pa2, b2, d4, f2, g2, h2 (10).

         B. Kg8, Qe7, Rf8, Ktb8, Pa6, b6, d5, f7, g7, h7 (10).

31. W   W. Kg1, Qd2, Ra1, e1, Pc2, c3, d4, f2, g4, h3 (10).

         B. Kc8, Qc7, Rf4, Bc6, Pa6, b7, d5, e4, e6, g7, h7 (11).

32. B   W. Kg1, Qd3, Rc1, e1, Bc2, e5, Ktf1, Pa2, b2, f2, g2, h3 (12).

         B. Kg8, Qd7, Ra8, d8, Be6, e7, Ktf6, Pa6, b5, d4, f7, g7, h7 (13).

33. B   W. Kd2, Qb2, Rf3, f4, Ba3, Pc2, c3, d4, e5, f2, h5 (11).

         B. Kc7, Qe6, Ra8, g8, Ktf5, Pb6, c4, d5, f7, g6, h6 (11).

34. W   W. Kg1, Qe5, Rd1, d4, Bf3, Pa2, b3, e3, f2, g2, h3 (11).

         B. Kg8, Qc5, Rd7, d8, Be6, Pa5, b6, d5, f7, g7, h6 (11).

35. W   W. Kg1, Qd1, Rb1, e1, Bd3, g3, Ktb3, f3, Pa2, b2, c3, d4, f2, g2, h2 (15).

         B. Kg8, Qd8, Ra8, f8, Bd6, d7, Kta4, c6, Pa6, b5, c7, d5, e6, f6, h7 (15).

36. B   W. Kc1, Qc2, Rd1, e1, Bd3, Ktc3, e5, Pa2, b2, d4, e3, f4, g2, h2 (14).

         B. Kb8, Qe7, Rd8, h8, Bd6, e6, Ktf6, Pa7, b7, c6, d5, f7, g7, h6 (14).

37.	B	W.	Kg1, Qd1, Ra1, f1, Be2, g5, Kte4, Pa4, b2, d4, f2, f6, g2, h2 (14).
		B.	Kc8, Qb6, Rd8, h8, Bb7, f8, Ktd7, Pa7, b4, c6, c4, e6, f7 (13).

38.	B	W.	Ke1, Qh7, Ra1, h1, Bd2, h5, Pa3, c2, c3, f2, g2, h2 (12).
		B.	Ke8, Qc5, Ra8, g8, Bc8, Kte7, Pa7, b7, d5, e5, f7 (11).

39.	W	W.	Kg1, Rc1, f1, Bg2, Ktc3, Pa3, b2, d4, e3, f2, f4, h2 (12).
		B.	Kh8, Rc7, c8, Bb5, Ktf6, Pa7, b7, d5, e6, f5, g7, h7 (12).

40.	W	W.	Kg8, Qd1, Rc3, f1, Ktd2, Pa2, b3, c4, d5, e3, f2, g3, h2 (13).
		B.	Kg8, Qc8, Ra8, f8, Ktd8, Pa7, b7, c5, d6, e7, f5, g6, h7 (13).

The Endgame

41.	W	W.	Kh8, Pc6 (2).
		B.	Ka6, Ph5 (2).

42.	W	W.	Kg5, Pa4, d4 (3).
		B.	Kb7, Pa6, a7, d5 (4).

43.	W	W.	Ke3, Pb2, b4, d5, g2, h3 (6).
		B.	Ke7, Pa6, b7, f6, g6, h6 (6).

44.	W	W.	Kc4, Pf4, g4 (3).
		B.	Kg7, Pf7, g6 (3).

45.	W	W.	Kd3, Pb5, e2, e4, g3, h4 (6).
		B.	Kf7, Pb6, d4, e5, e7, g6 (6).

46.	W	W.	Kg5, Qd4, Pg6 (3).
		B.	Ka5, Qe7 (2).

| 47. | W | W. | Ke2, Qd1, Pa4, b4, f2, f3 (6). |
| | | B. | Kh7, Qh2, Pb6, f4, g7, h4 (6). |

| 48. | W | W. | Kf4, Qb2, Pb5, d4, g2, h3 (6). |
| | | B. | Kf6, Qd5, Pb6, f7, g6, h5 (6). |

| 49. | W | W. | Kd3, Kta2, Pa3, b2, d4, e3, f2, g2, h2 (9). |
| | | B. | Kc6, Kte8, Pa4, b5, b6, d5, f6, g7, h7 (9). |

| 50. | W | W. | Kh1, Ktd5, Pa4, b2, f2 (5). |
| | | B. | Ke2, Ktf3, Pg4, h3, h5 (5). |

| 51. | B | W. | Kc3, Bc5, Pe3, f4, h4 (5). |
| | | B. | Kf3, Be6, Pb3, d5, g6, h5 (6). |

| 52. | B | W. | Kf4, Bc1, Pc5, d6, e5, h4 (6). |
| | | B. | Kd5, Bd7, Pa4, b7, f5, h5 (6). |

| 53. | W | W. | Kd3, Bg7, Pb3, c4, e4, f3, h3 (7). |
| | | B. | Kf7, Ktd8, Pb4, c5, f4, g5, h5 (7). |

| 54. | B | W. | Kg3, Bd7, Pg2, h4 (4). |
| | | B. | Kf6, Rh1, Pg6, h5 (4). |

| 55. | W | W. | Kd2, Re7, Pe4, f2, h6 (5). |
| | | B. | Kh8, Rd4, Pd3, g4 (4). |

| 56. | W | W. | Kf5, Rd5, Pe5, g4, h5 (5). |
| | | B. | Ke7, Ra7, Pg7, h6 (4). |

| 57. | W | W. | Kf4, Rc3, Pe4, g5, h4 (5). |
| | | B. | Ke6, Rc8, Pc4, g6, h5 (5). |

| 58. | W | W. | Kg3, Rf1, Pa4 (3). |
| | | B. | Ke4, Rb4, Pa5, g5 (4). |

| 59. | B | W. | Kd2, Rg5, Kte5, Pa5, f6, g4 (6). |
| | | B. | Kf8, Ra3, Bc8, Ph7 (4). |

| 60. | W | W. | Kh8, Pe3, g5, h5 (4). |
| | | B. | Kf5, Bc2, Kte1, Pc5, e6 (5). |

Trends in the Chess World

The Fate of "Living" Chess

Living chess does not refer to a game with live pieces but to chess played by living people. If the machine can beat a grandmaster at the chessboard, if a non-living chess player can beat a living player, will not living chess expire? Will not chess masters be out of work? A certain uneasiness on the part of the chess masters in the face of such a prospect seems reasonable. One must assume, however, that the interests of the masters will not suffer.

Living chess has no need to die. The development of automobiles and motorcycles has not decreased the public's interest in track athletics; millions of spectators fill the stands in the stadiums to look at runners. The track is the place for deciding who is the fastest runner in the world; chess contests will continue as before to decide who is the best player in the world.

All the same, we can put the question more clearly. People have always known that they are not the swiftest runners in the world; many animals run faster than man; but people have always thought that man was more intelligent than any other organism. Therefore man easily accepted the appearance of the automobile, but feels pain at the thought of "thinking" machines.

The Chess Master as a Scientist

When a machine can beat a living player, there will be a demand for grandmasters in scientific research institutes. If the theory we have expounded is correct, then for the first time in chess history it will be possible to analyze and compare (both as to style and to strength) the games of the great masters of many ages—for instance, Morphy, Steinitz, and Alekhine. When playing for annihilation of pieces, chess players can be distinguished only by the distance of the horizon (by the greater or lesser number of half-moves contained in the map). In playing for a change in the attack (or negation) functions (see p. 22), they may show a distinction that is finer than that of horizon distance alone. Although chess historians before now have had to compare players of different periods on a subjective basis, we may now be able to use objective criteria.

If research of this kind is started, grandmasters and masters will be needed as participants. Whenever mathematicians attempt to translate chess algorithms into programs, they will need the help of grandmasters.

In any case chess masters will find themselves entering into the role of scientific research workers. This will be no very sharp change of character for them; every chess player must to some extent become a research worker if he wishes to become a master.

There is another field in which the master can be useful. When the machine begins to play chess there will be an opportunity to compare the machine game (where the method of play and all the calculations will be known to the investigator) with the grandmaster's game, and thus learn how man thinks. In this instance the master will be assigned the humble role of the experimental guinea pig; but it will be a wholly safe and highly important role. We may assume that the grandmaster will not only have work to do, but will also have new and exciting prospects. He must rise even earlier in the morning, so as not to be late for the work.

The Difference Between Chess Player and Scientist

Why was Wiener not a good chess player? Why could he not foresee moves by his opponent that were obvious? Shannon put these questions to me in 1965, and I could only shrug my shoulders. How could I know? The question is extremely serious. No one can doubt the intelligence of Norbert Wiener, a very great scientist. Nor can one doubt the intelligence of Alekhine, a very great chess player. Why was Wiener helpless at chess and Alekhine at mathematics?

I think we can now form a hypothesis as to the reasons for Wiener's errors at the chessboard. A chess player, pondering a move, uses no auxiliary aids. He may take advice from no one. He may not consult a book for counsel. He may not look at notes, nor at pieces of paper with calculations on them. He is strictly limited in his time for thinking. He may not retract a move. A chess master's algorithm for play does not change. The chess player has only one right—to construct and analyze (mentally!) the map of the position and come to a decision. If we may use a computer as an analogue of the brain, there can be no doubt that what is needed is an extraordinary development and an exceptional training of that portion of the brain which is dedicated to operational memory and to calculation.

To the scientist these qualities of the chess warrior are probably not necessary, since the scientist has the right to solve his problems without haste, to correct errors, to take such advice and counsel as he needs, use handbooks, calculating machines, etc. Above all, he must have the ability to do research. And what is that? It seems likely that it is the ability to solve a variety of problems. For this, one needs (to return to the analogy with the computer) the ability to construct and test programs of differing character.

General Questions in the Theory of Management Systems

As we have already noted, the tasks that a management system must accomplish fall into three classes: 1) getting information, 2) using it to arrive at a decision, and 3) executing the decision.

Take, for instance, an elementary case of control—the method for regulating a synchronous machine. The control system has different sources (data units, transmitters) yielding information on the speed of the rotor, the current in the rotor, and the cosine of the stator circuit angle. This information is processed in a special regulator and the solution (data on the necessary magnitude and phase of the voltage at the brakes on the rotor winding) is given to the input of the executive organ—the power element.

These three elements in a management system (data units, data processors, and effectors) must be mutually compatible, otherwise the system may not work. Small children are not normally given matches and we can understand why. The data-gathering and logical capabilities of the child are unequal to the effector in the system (the box of matches); experience tells us that if such a "control system" begins to function accidentally, we are in for catastrophe.

Earlier in the history of mankind the logical possibilities for processing information which were open to man corresponded closely to his energy resources (the power of the effector organ). Things are different now. People have mastered the energy of the atom; the power of the effector organ has grown extraordinarily, but the power of the logical apparatus has scarcely changed. Therefore it is basically necessary to perfect man's ability to manage by a jump in his logical resources. The sooner this is done the better.

Man's part in control, in management, will appear to be limited, since there will remain to man only the setting of the task, the development of the program, and the choice among solutions recommended by the machine. And at the same time the power of control and management systems—looked at from the point of view of the correctness of the decisions arrived at—will grow at an unheard-of rate.

Some scientists fear that with the appearance of such "thinking" machines, machines that exceed man in logical ability, mankind may be enslaved or exterminated by them. To be sure, this is a sensational notion, but is such a peril thinkable? For a long time now mankind has built many types of machines that exceed the physical power of the human. And? In the ordinary life of people everything goes ahead prosperously (man suffers from the physical power of the machine only by accident or in time of war). Why? Because the machines have been properly designed. Why should it be otherwise with a "thinking" machine? The programs will be properly designed, and man will have a faithful and diligent helper.

Perhaps chess itself will prove to be a sharp tool that will carve out new paths for investigation.

At the present time a young mathematician, V. I. Butenko, is translating the algorithm discussed in this book into the language of the M-220 computer.[6] For the time being he is programming the standard and very important part of the algorithm. He is "teaching" the machine to determine the attack paths on a board filled with pieces, within a given horizon. He has had some successes: for instance, the determination of all shortest paths of the King from the square a4 to the square h4 (and there are 393 such paths) is made by the machine in something like a tenth of a second. The determination of all the attack paths (the assertions) in a three-half-move horizon for the position discussed previously, from the Botvinnik-Capablanca game (Fig. 22), required only 5 seconds.

---

[6] See Appendix A.

APPENDICES

APPENDICES

Appendix A

Preface to the Russian Edition

The reader will undoubtedly find this book most interesting. To begin with, it deals with the question of how a computer can play chess. Even more interesting, it was written by one of the greatest chess players of our times. And finally, the rules which the author has formulated by which machines can play chess were developed by analysis not only of his own games but also games of other chess masters.

In this book, M. M. Botvinnik takes critical issue on a series of questions with mathematicians who have developed and will develop programs for computerized chess play. The editor, a mathematician himself, is not in complete agreement with the author. He nevertheless took part eagerly in the work on the book because he considered it interesting not only for chess players and mathematicians, but also for psychologists and for everyone who knows chess even at the amateur level and knows mathematics at the high-school level.

It is worthwhile to pause for a moment to see what kind of a machine it is that plays chess and how it does so. What we have in mind is the modern programmed digital computer and in particular the electronic computer. Such machines may be thought of as complicated automata which consist of a number of interconnected components: control, memory, operational portions, input and output devices. Information can be fed to a program-controlled machine and stored in its memory in the so-called alphameric form (that is, in the form of letters and numbers). This information is of two kinds: commands and data. A program which controls the machine is a series of commands. The control portion of the machine fetches from the memory, one after another, the commands which make up the program, and causes the rest of the machine to carry them out. The control portion itself is subject to command as, for example, when it moves from one portion of the program to another under certain transfer commands.

The flexibility of the electronic computer derives from the fact that the order in which the commands are chosen can vary depending on the results of the operations performed, and also on the fact that the control information, as well as the data, are represented in alphameric form and can be subjected to processing by the machine. Modern programs work not only on the data but on the commands themselves and thus achieve an extraordinary flexibility.

To play chess, a machine proceeds as described below. A previously written program is fed in through the input device. Then the memory of the machine is loaded with data consisting of a description of the initial position of the chessboard. Next, the order of the moves is determined and this information is given to the machine. If the move belongs to the machine, it executes the program, calculates its moves, and announces the move through the output device (for example, an electric typewriter). At the same time, the machine calculates the new position and stores it in its own memory in place of the old position. It then halts (by a pre-planned command in the program).

The player who is contending against the machine makes the machine's move on the board and then makes his answer. The answer is described to the machine and fed into the memory through the input device. The start button on the machine is pushed, and the whole cycle begins again. If the first move belongs to the human player, the machine is told that the move does not belong to it, and it waits until the first move is made and given to it. The further course of the game is as just described. As we have already noted, the program is a series of commands, each of which, for every variation of the input data, defines uniquely the operation to be carried out by the machine, including the choice of the next command. Thus, the machine is merely the executor of a predetermined course of action described by the program. In other words, the program is a prescription which determines the actions of the machine, fed into the machine in machine language. The prescription, which uniquely determines the way in which the data will be handled for every concrete set of initial data, has been given the scientific name of "algorithm." We can say that a machine engaged in playing chess is implementing an algorithm for chess play.

An algorithm is not first written in machine language but in some other precise (formalized) language, say, mathematical symbolism: after this, the problem consists simply of translating the algorithm from one language to another. The translation of the algorithm to machine language is what is called programming.

It must be pointed out, however, that programming is not merely technical work. For each program that is written, one has to solve *de novo* a host of complicated problems, for example, defining the general organization of the program, specifying the locations of initial data and results in the memory, setting up editing mechanisms to guarantee the accuracy of the results (to prevent random errors from upsetting the calculating process), and so on.

Thus, to set up a machine to play chess one must first formalize the algorithm for playing, and to do this one must first make a thorough analysis of chess and come to the conclusion that such an algorithm is possible, and then, of course, write down the algorithm. The third step is the programming.

There is another way in which the machine can be made to play chess: to develop an algorithm by which the machine can learn to write its own algorithm, that is, an algorithm by which, on the basis of a series of games, the machine itself develops an algorithm for chess play and perfects it in the course of further games. The problem of developing a self-teaching program is extremely interesting.

In this book, we deal with a predetermined program which is an algorithm for play. People, of course, have been playing chess for thousands of years and have succeeded in learning a great deal. Obviously a machine would make progress only very slowly because of the limited experience it would have. It therefore appears useful to set up a machine algorithm which would make use of the enormous accumulation of human experience.

Many different algorithms can be written in a single formal language. These algorithms may be equivalent, that is, they may lead to identical results, although by different paths, or they may be non-equivalent. If by an algorithm for precise play we mean one that leads to the fewest number of moves to attain a given end, then two precise algorithms can fail to be equivalent only if in some position there are equally good paths for attaining the goal, for example, winning. Aside from algorithms for precise play, there may exist others which we can call algorithms for more or less satisfactory play.

Let us now look at the game of chess to see what the possibilities are for developing precise algorithms.

We shall show that in the course of a chess game only three kinds of positions can arise: 1) the position implies a win (given correct play); 2) the position is hopeless (given correct play on the part of the opponent); and 3) the situation given correct play leads to a draw. We shall show also that there exists an algorithm for best play in chess which, given a winning position, will win in the smallest number of moves, in a drawn position will not lose, and in a losing position will take the greatest possible number of moves before losing. If the opponent makes a mistake, then the algorithm will transform the situation into a better position.

At the same time we must emphasize the fact that such an algorithm exists only in the sense that it is possible. Up to now it has certainly not been developed and it is in practice impossible to write because it would demand an astronomical number of computing steps. Nevertheless, the fact that such an algorithm exists in principle gives grounds for hoping or believing that some time we may develop an effective algorithm for playing chess. We shall return later to the question of what grounds exist for such a hope.

First we must convince ourselves that both Black and White must necessarily agree on the nature of the position. To do this we shall show that the real game of chess is equivalent to a game which we shall call the White Game.

The White Game is played by giving each of two competing chess players a board of his own on which he plays White, and employing an assistant who, after each move made on one of the boards by White, moves the Black pieces on the other board in such a way as to form an image of the just-made White move as reflected in a mirror placed vertically down the center of the board (that is, as though left and right sides were interchanged by reflection).

Thus, in order to simplify matters we have changed the problem of studying the actual game of chess to the problem of studying the White Game. Now, a chess game played as the White Game is a sequence of positions. If these positions are numbered sequentially by attaching the integers "1" (for the initial position) "2," "3," etc., to them, then positions "1," "3," "5" and so on correspond to the first player (that is, the one who began the game), and positions "2," "4," "6," and so on belong to the second. In each of these positions White is to move.

A move may be thought of as a transformation of one position into the following position in accordance with the laws of chess. A game ending in a win for one side ends in a position in which White has given mate. A position in which Black has given mate cannot exist in the White Game. Thus we can see that in studying a position on the board we can limit ourselves to those positions that arise for White.

In the second stage of the analysis of the chess game we shall show that the number of different positions on a chess board is finite. Here we have to sharpen up the concept of position. By a position we shall mean the configuration of pieces on the board supplemented in certain instances by information about the fact that every chess position specifies the possibility of choosing a move which is the best. The meaning of the term "best move" will be made more precise a little later. Till then we shall say that it is a move corresponding to the shortest path that will attain our goal.

There must be two Kings on the board; besides the two Kings there must be other pieces whose number can range from zero to thirty. The number of distinct combinations of pieces, each of which consists of two Kings and other pieces, is equal to the number of choices of k elements from a total of 30. (The reader will have to recall this from his course in elementary algebra.) This number is traditionally noted by C_{30}^k and is calculated according to the formula

$$C_{30}^k = \frac{30 \cdot 29 \, [30 - (k-1)]}{1 \cdot 2 \ldots k} \, .$$

Each of these combinations can be distributed on the board in a very great number of ways, and in fact the number of ways is equal to the number of selections from a totality of 64 in lots of $k+2$. This number we shall denote here by A_{64}^{k+2} and we calculate it according to the formula

$$A_{64}^{k+2} = 64 \cdot 63 \ldots [64 - (k+1)].$$

Thus the overall number of possible distributions of chess pieces on the board is equal to

$$T = \sum_{k=0}^{30} C_{30}^{k} \cdot A_{64}^{k+2}.$$

However, among these configurations some have to be deleted because they cannot be reached in a chess game (for example, any configuration in which the Kings of both sides are under check or have been mated). Moreover, some of the configurations we have enumerated will be identical because we have supposed that all the pieces are distinct, whereas some of them (for instance, Pawns of the same color) are indistinguishable.

Rejecting the nonsense configurations (including those in which Black has given mate) and retaining only those that are distinct, we obtain a number which is less than T. We shall denote it by U.

Among the remaining configurations there exist some in which the King and one Rook or the King and both Rooks belonging to White are on their original squares. These configurations (denote the number of them by V) are not positions. In order that such a configuration be a position we have to add information that will tell us whether the King has already been moved, and if it has not, which if any of the Rooks has been moved.

It is clear that any of these configurations can occur under one of four conditions: 1) the King has already been moved, or both Rooks have been moved; 2) the King has not been moved and the first of the Rooks has not been moved; 3) the King has not been moved and the second Rook has not been moved; and 4) the King has not been moved and neither Rook has been moved. Thus, each such configuration corresponds to four possible positions. Therefore, the number of all chess positions supplemented by information as to whether or not White may castle can be calculated as

$$P' = U - V + 4V$$

or

$$P' = U + 3V.$$

Taking account also of Black's possibilities for castling, we obtain

$$P = P' + 3W$$

or

$$P = U + 3V + 3W$$

where $W < P'$.

Thus, as we have already noted, $V < U;\ W < U + 3V;\ U < T$. We thus have the inequality $P < 16\,T$, that is

$$P < 16 \sum_{k=0}^{30} C_{30}^{k} \cdot A_{64}^{k}.$$

Therefore the quantity P of all possible chess positions is finite since it is does not exceed a well determined, although very large, number.

The reader may say that the supplementary information we have set down concerning the prehistory of the configurations does not exhaust the supplementary information needed in order to properly choose a move, that is, so that the given configuration (together with this information) can be considered to be a chess position. He may say that it is necessary to know whether this position has been repeated a sufficient number of times or whether it is part of a series of positions that has been repeated one or two times. We reply that, for correct play leading by the shortest path to a win, the repetition of a sequence of configurations will not occur and therefore for our present purposes any such information is useless.

We thus convince ourselves that the number of possible chess positions is finite. This means that the chess positions could in principle be enumerated (although in fact, they cannot be as there are so many of them that eons would not suffice to count them).

Let us now suppose that each position has been written down on a separate slip of paper. We select every position in which White has been mated, and we assign it to the Class 0. On every slip corresponding to such a position we write down with a pencil "Class 0." Next we select every position in which if White is to move he can mate Black and we assign this to the Class 1. In the White Game, for every position of Class 1, there exists at least one move which would transform it into a position of Class 0. Then we select all those positions in which every move by White will yield a position of Class 1, and we number these "Class 2." This process can be continued until we have exhausted all our stock of positions. Every time we form a class with an odd number we shall include those positions which admit at least one move leading to a position with an even class number, less by unity than the number of the class that we are creating. In assigning a position to a class with an even number, we will include those positions admitting *only* moves leading to odd positions with a lower number, and among these a move leading to an odd position with a number one less than the number of the class we are setting up. After finishing this process (we denote the largest number obtained in forming this class by M) there remain a number of positions not yet assigned to any class, for example, positions containing a stalemate for White and certain others. These remaining positions we assign to Class $M + 1$.

From the classification process itself it is clear that if the chess player encounters a position belonging to a class with an odd number, n ($n \leqslant M$), then with correct play he can win in n half-moves (if his opponent plays in the best possible way) or he may win more quickly. The best move will be any which confronts his opponent with a position tabulated in the class $n - 1$ (which is even). If the player encounters a position with an even number ($n \leqslant M$), then given correct play on the part of his opponent, he cannot win. The best move protracts the defeat as long as possible. If he finds himself confronted by a position belonging to the class $M + 1$, the best move will be one which leads to a position belonging to the same class, that is, a move which preserves the drawing position. We observe that in any position there may be several best moves (they may be said to be "equally good").

This concludes our examination of the abstract game of chess. An arbitrary position in a chess game guarantees us, given correct play, either a win or (again given correct play), a draw, or given correct play on the part of the opponent, guarantees us defeat.

It is now easy to imagine how one would use a rule for best play (an algorithm for exact play in chess).

1. We must find our position among those that are listed in our catalogue. By consulting the index number of the class in which the position occurs we already know the outcome of the game.

2. We look over the available moves until we find a best one: that is, if we are in a class $M + 1$ position, one that leads to a position belonging to the same class, and if we are in a class n position with $n \leqslant M$, a move that leads to a position of class $n - 1$.

Using this simple rule, we will play in the best possible fashion.

If the number of positions that a chess player may encounter were not hyper-astronomically gigantic, the game would lose all interest! In fact, one would merely need to look up one's current position in a catalogue and with the aid of the same catalogue determine the correct move. Even if the correct move were not to be found in a catalogue but were to be derivable by a series of computations, the game would lose all interest. If our unrealizable rule for correct play were at some time to be replaced by a realizable rule, the death sentence would at once be passed on the game of chess.

M. M. Botvinnik, however, forecasts a different state of affairs in this book. He believes that computerized chess (and this means, really, the development of algorithms for chess play) will not lessen the interest that the game holds for us: this arises from the fact that, for today at least, nobody dreams of an algorithm for precise play, and there are no hopes for its practical realization.

Botvinnik compares the problem of playing chess to a number of problems which he calls "complex," problems for which exact solution would require so much working over of the input information that, in the present state of science and technology, no hope of a precise solution exists. Here he touches on the subject matter of a new scientific discipline which goes under the name of the *Theory of Complex Systems*. In the study of many real systems, some have been successfully described with the aid of algorithms, essentially as follows: the external influences on the system and the response of the system to these external influences are represented by a set of numbers; the rules of the system are described by an algorithm (a precisely formulated set of rules) which allows us under given external influences to describe the response of the system. If this is successfully done, the algorithm which describes the system dynamics is said to be a mathematical description (or map) of the system itself.

A system described by an algorithm can be automated: we can replace it by a collection of machines controlled by an electronic computer. This can be done, however, only if the algorithm is simple enough, if it does not demand too much time or too many memory cells for today's computers to cope with. When we come to systems (and not just to the solution of problems), the realization of an algorithm may imply the use of resources other than time and memory space; for instance, the energy output of the machines controlled by the algorithm, or the material consumed, etc. We may say that a complex system is an algorithm that demands for its realization more resources than we have. The basic problem in the theory of complex systems is to construct a system that is not complex and that has an effect close to that of the complex system under study.

Botvinnik holds chess to be a problem for a complex system; to solve it he applies what he calls the *horizon method*. This method is interesting not only in itself and for the theory of chess, but also for the theory of complex systems. We can be sure that there are significant problems far removed from those of chess to which an approximate solution can be found by these methods.

We must look a little more closely at the horizon method. The algorithm based on it is not an algorithm for exact play. The horizon, as Botvinnik conceives it, is not an absolute. It is specified by a number n, the maximum number of half-moves to be taken into account in analyzing a variation. It serves to select those pieces, on both sides, whose location and potentials must be analyzed in any given situation. Thus the horizon defines a "region" of play; this region contains those pieces of one's own that can attack an enemy piece in n half-moves or less, plus the enemy pieces that can be so attacked, plus the enemy pieces that can hinder the attack and the pieces of one's own that can support it.

So, instead of studying all the pieces on the board, we look at only those pieces that lie on branches within the horizon; instead of studying all possible moves available to our own pieces, we analyze only those moves that lie on attack paths, plus the moves of pieces that support or counter the selected attacks.

The horizon method lets us choose from all possible moves a comparatively small number and lets us limit our investigation to these selected few. During the analysis of the several variations, the horizon may change from one move to another. This is the radical difference between the horizon method and the methods for analyzing chess positions that have been used in computerized games up to now.

In 1950 Claude Shannon, an American mathematician, made some basic observations on the possible ways of mechanizing chess. He reduced the game, in essence, to the choice of a depth of analysis (number of half-moves) and the analysis of all possible moves up to the selected depth. This includes moves of one's own, all possible answers to those, and so on.

After constructing all the positions corresponding to the given depth of analysis (positions arising from one's own moves), one computes the value of an estimating function for each of them. Without going into detail, we need say only that one then chooses the move that yields the maximum value for the evaluation function under the condition that at each opportunity the opponent chooses the half-move that would minimize the value of the function.

This method for playing chess by machine was applied in the program by which the Soviet computer played against the USA computer in the match described in the first section of the book.

It is easy to see that an algorithm of this sort takes into account all the pieces on the board and the analysis is carried out over all possible moves, the interesting and the useless as well. The paths of the pieces are not distinguished as a coherent unity and are not looked at in themselves. Aside from this, the valuation function itself needs some looking at, since the algorithm tries to maximize it. This function is so chosen that it is increased by winning an opponent's piece, developing one's own pieces, getting a passed pawn, etc., and decreased by similar features in the opponent's play. Thus the valuation function takes into account a number of factors normally said by textbooks on chess to favor success—but they are far from decisive! Such a valuation function presupposes that the "weight" of a collection of these factors is equal to the sum of the "weights" of each of them. It fails in the endgame and chess players say that it is not supported by the analysis of the game that would be made by a chess master.

All by itself, the notion of a valuation function is without doubt correct. If the reader will agree that among all possible moves there are better and worse, he has already accepted the existence of a valuation function, whose value is greater for better moves and lower for poorer moves. The question is, however, how do we improve Shannon's function?

Shannon himself proposed his function only as an example. He remarked that a complete inspection of all possible moves and all possible answers to them would demand a formidable amount of machine time; he recommended not investigating all moves and all answers. McCarthy tried to follow this recommendation but did not succeed; his attempts are examined by Botvinnik in the latter's discussion of the computer chess match.

Properly speaking, both these fundamental ideas of Shannon's appear in Botvinnik's horizon method, which allows us to limit the number of variants of the game that we study and to use a valuation function in order to select the best move after analyzing the individual variants. But Botvinnik's function, as opposed to Shannon's, takes into immediate account only one factor: the gain of material, in the form of the tangible and intangible value of the pieces. All the other factors, such as the mobility of one's own pieces, the constriction of the enemy's, the appearance of advanced pawns, and so on, are automatically taken into account insofar as they affect the gain of material. In the horizon method, the survey of prospective variants is not carried out by looking ahead for a fixed number of moves, but rather by carrying the survey up to the point of either 1) establishing the uselessness of the particular variation, 2) establishing its usefulness, or 3) exhausting the alternatives available to the machine. The uselessness of a variation is relative, and the evaluation may change if the horizon is extended. An essential point is that where Shannon's method deals with the whole board and all the pieces on it (both when inspecting moves and when computing the value function), Botvinnik deals only with pieces that fall within the horizon.

For a sufficiently distant horizon (that is, for a large enough machine) the horizon method reduces to the analysis of all the attack paths of all one's own pieces. It then becomes a kind of algorithm for exact play, which cannot be classed with the methods used in the match between the Soviet and American computers.

One cannot say that Botvinnik's method is completely worked out. There are positions in which his algorithm appears to offer no clear prescription for the choice of move. A whole string of questions remain that can be solved only when Botvinnik's ideas have been realized in a program and run on a machine. In particular, the usefulness of the coding tables described in the book needs to be tested in this way.

The use of the coding tables to define the paths of the pieces will be justified, or not, depending on whether it is economical, whether it saves machine time and memory space. If it is economical it will generate more paths.

Although some of the details may be incomplete, Botvinnik's work has been thoroughly thought through with respect to the basic method. Trial and refinement is what it needs now.

N. A. Krinitskii

Appendix B

The Continental Chess Notation

Botvinnik's notation is not in common use in the United States. A brief explanation of it would therefore seem to be desirable.

Each square on the chessboard is designated by a letter and a number, corresponding to the file and the rank in which it lies. The files (the vertical columns) are indexed by lower-case letters, from a through h, beginning at White's left and ending at his right. The ranks (the horizontal rows) are numbered from 1 to 8, beginning on White's side and ending on Black's.

A move is indicated by listing the symbol denoting the piece moved, then the symbol for the initial square, an auxiliary symbol, the symbol for the terminal square. The notation is compressed as far as it can be; if one or both of the coordinates of the starting point can be deduced from other data, they may not be written out. Each move in a game is numbered; White's move is listed immediately following the number, then Black's, separated by a space. If White's move is not listed, as in the study of a variation, Black's move is preceded by three dots.

A hyphen between the symbols for the initial and terminal squares indicates a move. A colon indicates that a capture occurs on the terminal square. A plus sign following the listing of the move indicates that check is given to the opponent's King. Pawn moves are indicated by the omission of the symbol for the piece.

The game analyzed by Botvinnik in his first chapter opens as follows: 1. e2-e4 e7-e5 2. Ktg1-f3 Ktb8-c6 3. Ktb1-c3 Bf8-c5 4. Ktf3:e5 Ktc6:e5, and so on, or, in the cursive form, 1. e4 e5 2. Ktf3 Ktc6 3. Ktc3 Bc5 4. Kt:e5 Kt:e5. In the

notation commonly used in the United States these moves would be described as
follows:

	White	Black
1.	P-K4	P-K4
2.	Kt-KB3	Kt-QB3
3.	Kt-QB3	B-B4
4.	KtxP	KtxKt

or, in the cursive form, as 1. P-K4, P-K4; 2. Kt-KB3, Kt-QB3; 3. Kt-QB3, B-B4;
4. KtxP, KtxKt, and so on.

The Total Number of Chess Positions

Krinitskii derives an expression for the total number of different chess
positions, or more exactly, an upper bound for this number. His expression,
given on p.   71 for the number T, is

$$T = \sum_{k=0}^{30} C_{30}^{k} \cdot A_{64}^{k+2} .$$

The ratio of the term with index k to its successor, which we denote by R_k, has
the value $R_k = (k+1) / (30\text{-}k) (62\text{-}k)$. Except for high values of k, the ratio is
small; this means that in evaluating the series expression for T, only the last few
terms are significant. It turns out that the whole expression is equal to about 2.5
times the value of the last term, i.e., $T = 2.5 (64!) / (32!)$. Evaluating the
factorials in this expression by means of Stirling's formula, we find that T is of
the order of 10^{54}, and Krinitskii's upper bound for the total number of chess
positions is therefore 1.6×10^{55}.

Shannon, by a different process, estimates the number of chess positions and
arrives at 10^{43}. It makes no difference which estimate one takes. Either number
is so large as to be infinite for all practical purposes. Our hypothetical dictionary
of chess positions can neither be constructed nor consulted. Suppose, for
example, that we had a machine that could consult it at the rate of a million
positions per second. There are some 30 million seconds in a year; thus the
machine could look up 3×10^{13} positions a year and would be working for 3×10^{29} years to make a complete scan.

Nor can the machine analyze variations to any great depth. The number of
legal moves open to a player at each turn averages out to about 30 (according to
de Groot), so that the analysis of variations to a depth of two half-moves means
a study of 900 possibilities—say 10^3. Going to four half-moves means studying a
million variations. A modern computer may execute from 20,000 to a million
operations per second; if only a few tens or hundreds of operations are required
for the analysis of one variation, the computer might hope to play to a depth of

four half-moves in a reasonable time. But this is not deep enough for the important variations. Since we multiply the number of variations by 30 at each half-move, it is clear that restrictions on the number of variations considered must be introduced. This restriction is one of Botvinnik's main goals.

Computers

Those readers who find Krinitskii's account a bit brisk can get a basic description of the nature and functioning of electronic computers from IBM's *Introduction to IBM Data Processing Systems.* Form F22-6517-2. Ivan Flores' *Computer Programming* and Maurice Halstead's *Machine Independent Computer Programming* are also of interest to an advanced and diligent general reader.

The M-220, for which Butenko is programming Botvinnik's algorithm, is a Soviet computer capable of about 20,000 three-address operations per second. (In a three-address machine, a single operation means "get data from cell A, do something to it, and store the result in cell B"; in a single-address machine the fetching and storing are done by separate commands. The word "operation" therefore has a different meaning in the two different cases. A three-address operation is equivalent to something like 2.5 single-address operations.) The M-220 compares with a machine capable of 50,000 single-address operations per second.

MAC Hack VI was run on a Digital Equipment Corporation PDP-6. Greenblatt estimates that in this application the average speed was 200,000 single-address operations per second. The machine needed, on the average, 72 seconds to compute a half-move, i.e., it went through 14 million operations while making up its mind. The actual time, in one tournament game, varied between 111.7 seconds, while deciding to move P-KR4, and 4.5 seconds, while deciding to recapture after losing a Rook.

The Botvinnik-Butenko program required the equivalent of 250,000 single-address operations to compute all the attack paths in a complex position, with a three-half-move horizon (Fig. 22). This datum is not directly comparable with the Greenblatt data, since we do not know how much time will be needed by the Botvinnik-Butenko program to complete its decisions once the attack paths are computed.

Game Trees

A game tree is a conceptual device, representable in the form of a graph that resembles a tree. It is used for keeping track of the relations among the positions that may occur in a game.

Each position is represented by a dot (supposedly identified by an index of some sort; the assignment of the index may be done in an arbitrary fashion). If Position B can be reached from Position A by a legal move, a line is drawn between the two corresponding dots, and A is said to be the *ancestor* of B (or predecessor) and B a *descendant* (or successor) of A. Since the relation is one-sided (from A to B), some indication of the direction is required. We may think of the line as having an arrowhead pointing from A to B, or we may think of ancestor positions as being placed above the corresponding descendant positions, as in a family tree. This latter representation would do for a game such as bridge, in which no move is reversible; in chess, certain positions may be repeated after a number of moves, and these are descendants of their own descendants, so that the arrow notation is required.

In practice, no sane person would attempt to draw a complete game tree for even four half-moves in the game of chess, because he would not attempt to draw a million or so arrows. In all but the simplest situations, the game tree must be thought of purely as an aid of language and thought.

Decision Trees

A decision tree represents a game in which the half-moves alternate between an intelligent player and an opponent known as Nature, who makes moves that are not planned. Many examples of one-move or two-move trees come readily to mind. Trivially, the decision as to whether or not to protect against the weather: in setting out from the house, how should one dress? If protected against a heavy rain, the clothing is cumbersome; otherwise, one is comfortable, provided it does not rain. The tree looks like this:

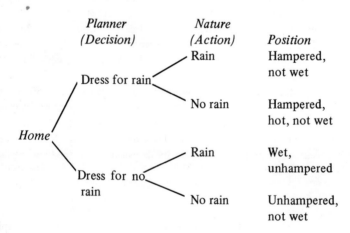

By some means or other, the planner assigns probabilities to Nature's action and values to the positions; he then calculates the expected value of various courses of action and makes up his mind according to one or other predetermined strategy *(protect against the worst, take a chance, etc.)* which he has reduced to quantitative form.

This example is trivial, in that the decision is of no great consequence and the horizon is set at two-half moves. A military decision, an investment decision, or a personal decision affecting one's life in a major way will be much more grave and difficult, in that the consequences are important and the horizon is much more distant. The analysis is correspondingly much more complex. If there are only five half-moves on either side, and each involves only two descendants, the final set of outcomes will contain 1024 points. One cannot deal intuitively with so many possibilities. Some method of simplification, such as discussed in this book, must be found, because important decisions should not be taken blindly.

A basic account of the nature and use of decision trees is given in John Magee's *Decision Trees.*

Long-Range Planning

The function of a long-range plan is to provide a guide to present action. No decision can be made in the future; postponement of action means deciding not to act, and the decision not to act is a current action. Since, as Botvinnik observes, the task facing the managers of an organization is inexact (the amount of information to be assimilated and used as a decision base is larger than the managers can grasp and use), some method of simplification is required. Viewed in this light, a long-range plan should provide criteria for simplification, for selecting the important information and for neglecting the unnecessary; it should also provide techniques for evaluating projected outcomes and methods, corre-lated with the techniques, for finding and assessing the paths by which the outcomes are to be reached.

Botvinnik's concept of position play, in which the goal is to strengthen oneself rather than to gain immediate material advantage, deserves emphasis, study, and formal incorporation into the process of long-range planning. This concept, as Botvinnik expounds it, is based on a model of the manager's functional environment. The evaluation function and the nature and influence of the competitive factors are supposedly known, so that the meaning of "strengthening one's position" can be explicitly defined.

There seems to have been little formal work along these lines. The state of the art in 1963 is summarized in a collection of papers, *Long Range Planning for Management*, edited by David W. Ewing of the Harvard Business Review. Good managers have obviously made tacit use of this notion, but tacit use is much different from explicit and formal development.

Appendix C

The Value of the Pieces

The *tangible value* of a piece is a number representing its material strength, measured in units of a Pawn. The values adopted in this book are those suggested by Shannon:

Piece	Tangible Value
King	200
Queen	9
Rook	5
Bishop	3
Knight	3
Pawn	1

Since the King cannot be yielded or captured, it has no exchange value in itself. But a very high tangible value has to be assigned to it, since if it is "lost" the game is lost, so that its value is infinite. The number 200 is chosen simply as a very large number, higher by far than the sum of the values of all the other pieces. The remaining values are those that have emerged from chess experience and are generally accepted as good approximations to the material worth of the pieces.

The tangible values of White pieces are denoted by real numbers; the values of the Black pieces are denoted by imaginary numbers. The symbol j represents $\sqrt{-1}$ in accordance with engineering usage. (The multiplicative properties of j are not used; only the fact that its absolute value $|j| = 1$ is used.)

The *intangible value* of a piece may vary throughout the game. At any moment, it is equal to the sum of the material values of the enemy pieces that it has captured. The algorithm must look ahead and must therefore calculate intangible values that result from hypothetical moves. The definition of intangible values is compatible with this purpose.

The Path of a Piece: α-squares and β-squares

The calculations relating to an attack must be based on a specific *attack path*, consisting of squares through which the attacking piece must pass to reach its object. A square on which it must come to rest is called an α-square. A square that it traverses without stopping is called a β-square.

The Place-Function

The place function f is defined at the α-squares of an attack path or retreat path; it is a logical function, having the value 1 at a specified square if that square is free and secure, and having the value 0 otherwise. (The same refers to β-squares. When a piece is placed on a β-square it becomes an α-square.) It is not defined and is not needed, in connection with any squares other than α-squares; it is evaluated for a specific attack or retreat and has no meaning except by reference to the action in question.

The Attack-Functions

The function ψ has the value 0 until the piece under attack is captured; at the moment of capture, it has the value 1.

The functions F and Θ (for White and Black, respectively) have the value 1 if the attack is inescapable, and have the value 0 otherwise.

The Formulae

The Attack Functions   The functions F and Θ are distinguished by different symbols only for convenience, to keep the calculations for White separate from those for Black. They are defined by the same formula.

$$F = \Pi \, (1 - f_k) \cdot \Pi f_i \qquad\qquad (1)$$

(The symbol Π, for *product*, means that the factors following it are to be multiplied together.) The indices k refer to the α-squares of the paths by which the piece under attack may hope to retreat; if any one of these squares is free and secure, the corresponding f_k has the value 1, and the factor $(1 - f_k)$ has the value 0. Then F has the value 0. If any one of the α-squares of the attack path is encumbered by a piece of the same color as the attacker, or if it is insecure (if a piece that comes to rest on it can be captured), the corresponding place-function

f_i has the value 0, and so F has the value 0. If none of these conditions exist, then $F = 1$, and then also, the attack cannot be warded off or avoided.

The function ψ is defined by the formula

$$\psi = \frac{1}{2} \cdot \left(1 - \frac{2n_{ir}-1}{|2n_{ir}-1|}\right) \tag{2^2}$$

Here i denotes the square on which the attacking piece rests, r denotes the square on which the attacked piece rests, and n_{ir} is the number of half-moves needed for the attacking piece to go from the α-square i to the α-square r.

The Control or Blockade Function   The control or blockade function ρ for a specified α-square has the value 0 if the square can be controlled or blockaded; otherwise it has the value 1. It is defined by the formula

$$\rho_n = \frac{1}{2} \cdot \left(1 - \frac{n_{ik}-n_{rk}+a}{|n_{ik}-n_{rk}+a|}\right) \tag{3'}$$

Here n_{ik} is the number of half-moves needed for the piece at the α-square i to go to the α-square k of the trajectory, and n_{rk} is the number of half-moves needed for the piece that is to control or blockade the α-square k to get there from the α-square r. For control, $a = 2$; for blockade, $a = 0$.

The Exchange Function   The exchange function τ is a measure of the gain or loss resulting from a capture. It is defined by the formula

$$\tau_m = \frac{1}{2} \cdot \left(1 + \frac{m+0,1}{|m+0,1|}\right) \tag{3''}$$

If the gain m is negative, $\tau_m = 0$; otherwise $\tau_m = 1$.

The Place-Function

$$f = \tau_m + \rho_n - \tau_m \cdot \rho_n \tag{3}$$

The Skirmish Function   Let m_k denote the material gain on the final square of an attack path, and let m_i denote the minimum value of the gain on any intermediate α-square. Then

$$\tau_{\Delta m} = \frac{1}{2} \cdot \left(1 + \frac{m_i-m_k+0,1}{|m_i-m_k+0,1|}\right) \tag{4'}$$

$$\varphi = 1 - \rho_n - \tau_{\Delta m} + \rho_n \cdot \tau_{\Delta m} \tag{4''}$$

Then the tangible value attacked is

$$m = m_k \cdot \psi_k + \Delta(m, \psi) \cdot \varphi_i$$

where

$$\Delta(m, \psi) = m_i \cdot \psi_i - m_k \cdot \psi_k \tag{4}$$

The Negation Function   The intangible value of a first-order denial of a place-function belonging to an attack path is

where

$$0_1 = -M_0 \cdot \psi_0 \cdot \Delta_i F_0 \cdot \psi_{1i} \cdot F_{1i} \tag{5}$$

$$\Delta_i F_0 = F_0 \left(1 - f'_{0i}/f'_{0i}\right).$$

The value of the denial of a denial at the α-square k is

$$O_2 = - M_0 \cdot \psi_0 \cdot \Delta_i F_0 \cdot \psi_{1i} \cdot \Delta_k F_{1i} \cdot \psi_{2k} \cdot F_{2k} \qquad (6)$$

Computation of the Attack Path Function   The attack path function F_0^R is the result of negation path functions.

$$F_0^R = \prod^h (1 - f) \cdot \prod_{i=1} \left\{ f_{0i} + \Delta f_{0i} \cdot \prod_{k=1}^q \left\{ f_{1k} + \Delta f_{1k} \times \right.\right.$$

$$\left.\left. \times \prod_{m=1}^p [f_{2m} + \Delta f_{2m} \cdot \prod_{n=1}^r (f_{3n} + \Delta f_{3n} \cdot \prod_1^s \cdots \right.\right\} \qquad (7)$$

On the question of multiple exchanges, see the Author's Preface to this edition.

Computation of τ_m   An exchange is favorable for White if

$$\Sigma \,|\, jN \,| - \Sigma \,|\, M \,| \geqslant - \,|\, jN \,| \cdot \theta \qquad (8')$$

and for Black if

$$\Sigma \,|\, jN \,| - \Sigma \,|\, M \,| \leqslant \,|\, M \,| \cdot F \qquad (8'')$$

The General Exchange Formula   An analysis of a variation should be continued by White as long as

$$\Sigma \,|\, jN \,| - \Sigma \,|\, M \,| \geqslant - \Sigma \,|\, jN \,| \cdot \theta - \Sigma \,(1 - \theta) \cdot \,|\, jN \,| \cdot \gamma \qquad (9')$$

where

$$\gamma = \frac{1}{2} \cdot \left(1 - \frac{\Delta q + 0,1}{|\, \Delta q + 0,1 \,|} \right) \qquad (10)$$

Black should continue the analysis of a variation as long as   (9'')

The Condition for Mobilizing Auxiliaries   If q denotes the number of α-squares in an attack path at which $f = 0$, and ν is a number limiting the complexity of the problem, then the bringing in of other pieces should be considered if

$$\Sigma \,|\, jN \,| - \Sigma \,|\, M \,| \leqslant \Sigma \,|\, M \,| \cdot F + \Sigma \,(1 - F) \cdot \,|\, M \,| \cdot \gamma \qquad (9'')$$

Types of Value

Type I.   Value of pieces already removed from the board.

Type II.   Value of pieces certain to be captured, in a play for annihilation.

Type III.   Value of pieces certain to be captured within the positional horizon.

Type IV.   Value of pieces on paths for which the path-functions differ from 1.

The Position Estimate

If

$$q < \nu \qquad (11)$$

White may find it advantageous to make a positional sacrifice. If the sign is reversed, the position favors Black.

Appendix D

Bibliography

There are more than 10,000 titles, in and out of print, on the subject of chess. The current catalogue of books in print lists about 250. In the field of artificial intelligence, there are more than 2000 papers and books. The number of papers on computers and computing is already immense and is growing daily. Only in the field of long-range planning is there relatively little published material.

The reader who wishes to explore the literature is in the same position as Botvinnik's parachutist, who lands in a bog and has to take some immediate action. This bibliography is intended only to tell him where he may find a few hummocks and a map or two. It does not pretend to do more.

The Game of Chess

In the very unlikely event that a reader unfamiliar with chess may have made his way to this point, we should note that there are introductory books by Chernev, Fine, Golombek, Horowitz, and Reinfeld, among others.

Statements of principles can be found in:

Capablanca, J. R. *Chess Fundamentals*. New York: David McKay Co., 1967.

Euwe, M. *The Development of Chess Style*. New York: David McKay Co., 1967.

Fine, Reuben. *Lessons from My Games*. New York: David McKay Co., 1958.

Nimzovich, Aron. *My System*. New York: David McKay Co., rev. ed., n.d.

Reti, Richard. *Modern Ideas in Chess*. New York: Dover Publications, n.d.

Spielmann, Rudolf. *The Art of Sacrifice in Chess*. New York: David McKay Co., 1951.

Tarrasch, Siegbert. *The Game of Chess*. New York: David McKay Co., n.d.

Chess and the Mind

de Groot, Adriaan. *Thought and Choice in Chess.* New York: Basic Books, 1966.
    A fundamental book, with an extensive bibliography; de Groot is a psycholo-
    gist and a Master chess player.
Fine, Reuben. *The Psychology of the Chess Player.* New York: Dover Publica-
    tions, 1967. A study of the psychoanalytic factors at work in the chess
    player, with analytical sketches of nine players of world-champion rank. Fine
    is a Grandmaster and a professional psychoanalyst.

Computers and Chess

The basic paper is Shannon's:
Shannon, Claude. *Programming a Computer for Playing Chess.* Philosophical
    Magazine, Vol. 41, March, 1950. This paper has been reprinted in *Computers
    and Thought* (see listing below) and in *The World of Mathematics* (Vol. 4)
    New York (Simon and Schuster) 1962.
Also of interest:
Greenblatt, Richard D., Eastlake, D. E., III, and Crocker, S. D. *The Greenblatt
    Chess Program*, Proceedings, AFIPS Fall Joint Computer Conference, 1967,
    pp. 801-10.

Further references will be found in de Groot's bibliography and in the
extensive bibliography published in *Computers and Thought.* References to
recent and current papers will be found in *Computing Reviews,* published by the
Association for Computing Machinery (ACM).

Artificial Intelligence

Carne, E. B. *Artificial Intelligence Techniques.* Washington, D.C.: Spartan
    Books, 1965.
Feigenbaum, E. A. and Feldman, J., eds., *Computers and Thought.* New York:
    McGraw-Hill, 1964. A collection of papers, including a reprint of Shannon's
    basic work. The classified bibliography is extensive and useful. There are
    thirty references to papers on game-playing by computer.
Yovitts, M. C., Jacobi, G. T. and Goldstein, G. D., eds., *Self-Organizing
    Systems—1962.* Washington, D.C.: Spartan Books, 1962.

Computers and Programming

Flores, Ivan, *Computer Programming.* Englewood Cliffs, N. J.: Prentice-Hall,
    1966.
Halstead, Maurice, *Machine Independent Computer Programming.* Washington,
    D.C.: Spartan Books, 1962.

Introduction to IBM Data Processing Systems, IBM General Information Manual, Form F22-6517-2, August 1964. Although the title of this latter publication refers to IBM equipment, the explanation of computer principles given in the manual is general and is applicable to a wide variety of computers.

The first two texts are concerned with the principles of programming; although they do not require a specific background and are written as basic texts, the reader will need to be energetic.

Long-Range Planning

Ewing, David W., ed., *Long-Range Planning for Management.* New York: Harper & Row, 1964.

Magee, John F., *Decision Trees for Decision Making.* Harvard Business Review, July-August 1964.